I0415074

SORROWLAND

Political Satire

on

The Fall of America

Don Alexander

ACKNOWLEDGEMENTS

The author wishes to express appreciation to those who inspired this book.

To: Al Gore who invented the internet into which is being fed the sum total of human thought, scientific knowledge, current and historical events; to Barack Obama for proving that a native born Kenyan raised as a Muslim, educated as a communist, mentored by a black militant, and intimate associate of domestic terrorists can be elected President of the United States; to Fox News for telling it like it is; to Glenn Beck and Sean Hannity for fearless reporting; to Missouri University School of Law for demonstrating that law yields to threats and influence.

DEDICATION

To my wife, Elaine, who tolerated my moods, anger and

humor while laboring to describe the fall of America

Don Alexander

ABOUT THE AUTHOR

Don Alexander was born in 1939 in Truman, Arkansas
inside a sharecropper cabin where chickens could be seen
through the floor and a pan of foot washing water would
freeze under the bed during a frosty winter night. Don is
currently retired and lives with his wife Elaine in Rocky
Mount, Missouri on a cove of the Lake of the Ozarks. Don
and Elaine's son is a doctor and their daughter is a nurse.

Don's parents could not help him financially, so he worked his way through grade school and high school. He became keenly aware that he needed more education so he spent the next thirty years getting a triple Bachelor of Science Degree in business, psychology and political science plus a doctorate in law. While being exposed to education, he worked twenty-six years as a commissioned salesman, maintenance mechanic, dock hand, dock foreman, machining foreman, production foreman, police officer, industrial engineer, and general contractor. He spent twelve years on the road as a business consultant with various consulting firms and then ran his own consulting operation for six years. He studied Latin, Greek and Russian while being educated in physics, chemistry, astrophysics, biology, zoology, anthropology, archeology, and advanced mathematics including statistics and mathematical probability at Hannibal-Lagrange College, Washington University and the University of Missouri - Columbia. He has read and studied the same subjects from his teen-age years to age 74.

He has written 32 books and 2 screenplays which are available at **Amazon.com**

SYNOPSIS

This book is a political satire which tracks with facts and humor the presidential campaign of an African born Muslim communist for the presidency of the United States. Never in the history of humanity has such a monstrous fraud been committed upon any major nation using blatant perjury, fabricated birth certificate and personal history, dishonest news media and gullible followers to foist into presidential power a con artist with zero business expertise, zero economic background, zero leadership experience, zero understanding of military strategy or foreign policy and zero capacity for making top executive decisions within a critical time frame. Incredibly, such a monumental fraud has been perpetuated into a second term leading to bankruptcy of the United States, a global currency and a one-world government under a socialist dictator pursuant to the descent of the United States into the abyss of incompetence.

CHAPTER ONE

Chicago reflects both the beautiful and ugly face of America. The skyscrapers overlooking Lake Michigan along the magnificent mile of shops, offices, restaurants and hotels do indeed mirror the fast pulse of "the city that never sleeps." Chicago was the center of organized crime and home turf of Al Capone in the days when cops, prosecutors, and judges could be bought for as little as five grand.

In the private clubs and gourmet restaurants the political soul of Chicago is still auctioned off to the highest bidder. In the heyday of gang warfare the mafia murdered any one who dared to oppose the easy flow of forbidden booze, whores and gambling.

The sixteen county urban area includes twenty-seven smaller municipalities and a population approaching ten million. Chicagoland ranks third behind Houston and

Dallas-Ft. Worth in housing new and expanded corporate

facilities.

For more than a century Chicago served as Mark

Twain's "hog butcher of the world" where an endless flow

of hogs and cattle were converted into prime cuts. The

world famous Union Stockyards had been the heartbeat of

the Chicago Mercantile Exchange. It functioned as an

agricultural futures market amid the smokestacks where

Irish, Polish, German and Italian immigrants converted raw

materials into steel, petroleum derivatives and industrial

capital goods for substandard wages and tenement housing

on the south side of the city.

Slumlords and barkeepers waxed fat off the sweat of

those fleeing oppressive governments to chase the elusive

American dream. With the passing of time the unions drove

heavy industry to developing nations and Chicago

reinvented itself through value added services, financial

trading, higher education, logistics and healthcare.

The liberal and corrupt Democratic machine churned out

novice politicians who could be depended upon to fleece

the poor and repay favors showered upon them by their

party overlords. The "pay to play" political quagmire was

both transparent and flagrant where once elected and

fervently loyal to party bosses one could remain in office

until sudden or natural death. A team player with charisma

and benevolent visage might even move into the White

House.

Barry Osama was deemed a likely candidate to succeed

President Walker Hush but presented himself with

considerable negative baggage. Born a Muslim in Kenya,

Africa he would have to be reborn somewhere in the USA.

Perhaps, Hawaii where his mother settled after being

deserted by Barry's father who was then still married to a

native African.

The Democrats controlled Hawaii---a utopia for liberal politicians. The party faithful could be depended upon to create something as simple as a birth certificate. It would help though if Barry's paternal grandmother would stop telling local ministers that she attended Barry's birth in Mombosa and if the Kenya ambassador to the US would cease and desist telling American talk show hosts that Barry's birthplace in Kenya is sure to become a tourist attraction. It would help considerably if Barry could somehow make those official documents disappear he signed as a foreign student to get financial aid and to fly to Pakistan when it was illegal for Americans to travel to that country.

But, Barry was truly making serious progress by severing relations with his rabidly racist black pastor who railed against America for twenty years while Barry listened with rapt attention. He saw less of his terrorist buddy and ghost writer Willie Bombsetter and his communist mentor Josif Givmeall. Barry also avoided his good buddy Abdulla Tuckuen, a real estate con artist who slid some prime real estate Barry's way for a fraction of its market value.

Moreover, Barry had served notice on his Muslim relatives not to come around too often until after his inauguration and then they could wine and dine on the American taxpayer while plotting the demise of Israel.

Although weighed down by his checkered background, Barry still would be easier to foist on the homosexuals, abortionists, evolutionists, atheists and lip service Christians than somebody like Senators Barney Smirk, Harry Heapiton, Chris Gimme, Nancy Tearieye, Bobbie Blamet, or Charles Rakitin.

Yeah, Barry was a little soiled but he could carry 95% of the black vote, virtually all the homosexuals, the vast majority of abortionists and evolutionists, and super rich

wannabe dictators like Georgie Sorrow. The left wing

media would fawn over Barry while he read professional

speechwriters' prose from a mini-teleprompter and

ridiculed the opposition.

 Yes, indeed! Barry would be the ideal candidate if he just

learned to avoid public snapshots with communists, tax

cheats, domestic terrorists, Muslim radicals, ex-cons,

obvious racial bigots, and slumlords. The fickle big city

voters were hooked on government handouts with no

income tax liability. Barry would promise them more of the

same with a little bonus from Uncle Sam to jump state the

sluggish economy. The poor, the ignorant and the

unemployed were solidly behind the man from Mombosa.

The only officials who could challenge his birthplace were

Democratic demagogues who could convince John Q

public that all those demanding verification of Barry's birth country were simply racial bigots who hated all blacks and certainly did not want one in the White House.

Barry Osama deftly stepped around two Yellow taxis partially blocking the intersection of State and Wacker as he headed for the private club in the Bank of America Building located at 115 South LaSalle Street. Some of the upper floors were still undergoing renovation made necessary by the December 2004 fire which ravished the 29th and 30th floors for lack of a proper sprinkler system proving once again that in Chicago a little payola trumps public safety.

Barry admired his athletic figure and benevolent smile reflecting from the store windows along Wacker Avenue. His salt and pepper parents had blessed him with Negro coloration and white features. His only distracting physical negative were his overly large ears.

Willie Bombsetter checked his watch the seventh time in

twenty minutes while scanning the club entrance for his

lunch companion. Willie was showing his age but still

looked distinguished in his hand tailored gray business suit,

horn rim glasses, pink silk shirt and black tie. But time had

converted his muscles to flab which tumbled over his belt

and wobbled under his pointed chin. His gray hair, steel

blue eyes and hawkish nose conveyed the impression of

one who could run for public office in Chicago.

Willie stifled a belch triggered by his scotch and soda

while helping himself to a handful of nuts from a courtesy

bowl. He had developed admiration for Barry's eloquence

and quick wit. But the candidate needed someone more

mature to help map out a campaign strategy to attract

donations from the radical liberals and anti-America

element permeating Illinois' vaunted halls of higher

education. Barry and Jemama Osama were personal friends

and close neighbors. Willy and his wife, Beatrice, had

hosted Barry's party announcing his candidacy for Illinois

senator and donated $2,500 toward his campaign financing.

It did not bother the candidate nor his wife that Willy

and Beatrice were confessed domestic terrorists who

murdered cops. They bombed government buildings amid

the hippie protests against law and order while American

soldiers were dying in the jungles of Vietnam. Neither did

they object to Willy publicly trampling the American flag

after being freed by a legal technicality after he confessed

to murder and mayhem.

Barry and Jemama had a good laugh about him beating

the system and becoming a socialist professor to

indoctrinate simple minded students. Willy was Barry's

ghost writer of a book describing Barry's quest for

intellectual achievement in the footsteps of his communist

father.

Barry exited the elevator directly across from the club

entrance and strode confidently to Willie's table. The white

coated waiter with curly black hair and manicured beard

saw him coming and ambled to the table to take his drink

order. Willie pushed his chair back and stood up with his

right hand extended.

"Afternoon, Senator. It's always a pleasure to dine with

you," Willie fawned as Barry shook his hand, took a seat

and turned to the waiter.

"Scotch and water, Jerry; and fix Mr. Bombsetter

another." Jerry headed for the bartender and Willie grinned

at Barry.

"Did you get your invitation from Sorrow?"

"Yes, I did. Said he has invited a couple dozen high

rollers who want me in the oval office. He also indicated

his total support and willingness to coerce everybody

indebted to his generosity."

"Wow!! That could be worth worth up to a billion.

Think McPaign suspects you can out spend him more than

six to one?"

"I doubt it. He's too occupied polishing his war

medals and practicing his crippled arms waving on the

campaign trail. I'll let him continue believing I'm relying

on federal funding plus normal contributions until it's too

late for him to change strategy."

Bombsetter chuckled softly. "How did that fumbling fool

ever beat out the other Republican competition? That 'my

friends' opener of his reminds me of Hoover convincing

farmers to drown their hogs to prop up the price of bacon."

Barry sipped his scotch and glanced around the table.

"The Republicans are so disorganized we should capture

the House and Senate along with booting Hush back to his

tumbleweed ranch. Every time that moron shows his face

on TV the stock market takes a dive. Speaking of Wall

Street, how about Heiny Takmore? That fox pilfers the

treasury and gets a seven hundred million bonus from

Riskmo Taxu and all he has to do is finance them with

taxpayer money. Between Takmore and that thief

controlling the Fed's interest rate the dollar gets

manipulated to pour billions into their straw man shell

corporations."

Bombsetter leaned forward with an amused smirk.

"That's peanuts compared to what our take will be while

collapsing the economy and eliminating capitalism. By the

time we jack the unemployment rate up to twenty percent

or so, and fifteen million more immigrants get the vote, the

Republican party will be history and we radicals can steer

the starving citizens into a world government."

Barry's eyes danced with a mixture of glee and

contempt. "People who are politically illiterate and believe

their ancestors were monkeys will swallow anything

anyone says who doles out their daily bread and gives them

more idle time to make babies and keep abortionists busy."

Bombsetter flashed his toothiest grin. "Let's not forget your gay fans. Snuffing potential citizens in the womb plus same sex bed partners will certainly reduce the mouths we have to feed to buy votes. Kids don't vote and our Robin Hood image of taking from the rich and distributing to the poor will keep the welfare generation beholden to you. Regardless of how far the stock market falls, we can keep blaming Hush and his cronies and promising the hungry more government assistance until the dollar becomes worthless and the majority of Americans clamor for global citizenship."

Barry drained his glass and signaled Jerry for another round. "From there it's all downhill, Willie.

Across the street from Oak Street Beach at 140 East Walton Place, the Drake Hotel's famous Palm Court dining room was serving traditional English tea and gourmet

crackers topped with exotic caviar. The grandiose old hotel

had been refurbished in old world décor to provide

luxurious comfort. The former Rush Street neighborhood

had changed from rowdy clubs where nude dancers teased

big tips from repeat patrons to high class shops and

restaurants typified by the shops of Water Town Place

situated at 835 North Michigan Avenue.

Valerie Slumster was fastidious about her physical

appearance. At sixty-one she looked ten years younger

aided by exotic facial creams, massages, demanding

exercises and professional hair styling. Her dyed, flip-up

brunette curls, bleached teeth and pleasant curves blended

well with her pampered face and manicured hands. She

was quite wealthy from rental properties and had become a

major Chicago slumlord. Valerie was a liberal socialite

with very influential political ties in both Chicago and

Springfield.

She sipped her tea and watched David Yurnany wolf

down caviar laden crispy crackers. She blotted her thick

red lipstick with a napkin and queried David. "How are the

latest polls shaping up?

Yurnany had established a reputation as a political

campaign manager even with his nondescript appearance.

He was partially bald which did not enhance his squat

pudgy frame and round homely face. He nodded at their

waiter for more tea and turned his attention back to Valerie.

"We're skewing the percentages in our favor by targeting

mainly working class urban centers especially in the swing

states. We're creating the "bandwagon mindset" to

convince Conservatives and Republicans in Florida, Ohio,

Virginia, Colorado, North Carolina, Indiana and Montana

that Osama has a lock on the election. So, they might as

well stay home rather than stand in line to cast a futile

vote."

Yurnany grinned slyly. "Every major news network except Telitright News is backing Osama and parroting our propaganda. We're discrediting Telitright and convincing the public that they are obstructionists, red-necks, and racists. We'll denounce their pollsters as biased and prone to fabricate favorable results. The uneducated and government wards will believe the main stream media and the rest we have written off as hard core opposition who will soon become the irreversible minority. Once we get 51% of the voters on government handouts, they have to keep us in control to keep eating."

Valerie already knew everything Yurnany was doing as Osama's personal radical consultant but she raised her eyebrows and turned thumbs up in appreciation of his obvious brilliance in undermining both democracy and capitalism. Actually, Valerie has fared quite well under both. She paid to play in Chicago and became exceedingly wealthy by buying distressed real estate and converting it into low income housing. The more unemployment and people forced onto the welfare rolls the more her investments mushroomed.

In addition, she had cultivated a trusting relationship with the Osamas and would share in the thievery while capitalism self-destructed. Barry looked to her for advice on the most deceptive schemes to increase the pool of voters being convinced that socialism is better than individual incentives when the majority is hindered by laziness and lack of education. She squinted at Yurnany and wrinkled her brow. "Are we getting enough support from Ivan Stylin at WOWU and Imma Boxstuffer at Forenborn? Especially in the swing states?"

Yurnany swallowed a mouthful of caviar and swigged his tea. "They've been following our game plan conscientiously so far. Workers of the World Unite banners

are being handed out at all WOWU local offices and

workers have contributed over twelve million as of this

week. Imma has ground workers in every swing state

paying low income people to register to vote; some as

many as seventy times at twenty dollars per cycle."

Yurnany again grinned with confidence. "The ground

workers are being paid a lucrative incentive based on

volume. Total registered voters are being inflated by at

least fifteen percent and a lot of our bogus registrations will

become votes through fictitious addresses in different

precincts, perhaps enough for us to carry the states. In any

event, the multiple registrations will be more effective than

rigging the polls to woo Conservatives and discourage

Republicans. Barry says don't worry about the expense.

Georgie Sorrow is good for at least a billion.

Upon returning to his private office, Barry Osama called Governor Ron Blowharder on his satellite cell phone. The Illinois Governor answered his secure phone on the third ring: "Governor Blowharder......."

"Senator Osama, Ron. Got your note from Bombsetter that you have a candidate for my seat in the Senate when I move to Pennsylvania Avenue. What's my seat worth?"

"A cool million from Sambo Mellon plus another half million from Reverend Mellon. Fleecing the flock is a rewarding task. You satisfied with Sambo?"

"Yeah. He's okay. We'll just keep him on a short leash until he learns how to pay to play. The Feds still snooping around?"

"Last time I checked. No problem. Those bozos couldn't find a hound tied to a tree in their own back yard. What's more.....the federal prosecutor can be bought for as little as a hundred grand. Right now he needs to find his kid a good lawyer. The lad got busted selling coke on campus. Dumb

like his dad."

"Take the money, Ron. Gotta run. Talk again soon."

Barry punched the off key and beckoned a welcome to

Ivan Stylin from WOWU who had suddenly appeared in

the doorway. "Hey, Ivan. Good to see you. Come on in."

The communist president of WOWU's 2.1 million service

employees union smiled pleasantly and took a seat opposite

the future president of the United States.

He lit up a cigar and offered one to Osama who clenched

it between his teeth while Stylin fired it up.

"We're doing better than anticipated, Senator. You're

going to get 99% of 2.1 million votes plus at least 25

million to help out with campaign expenses. We're making

sure that all of our people both vote and contribute."

Osama grinned widely, kicked back and raised his feet

onto the glass topped executive desk. "Never doubted you

for a second, Ivan. You wanna keep running WOWU or take a spot in my cabinet?"

Stylin looked more like an undertaker than president of one of America's largest union organizations. His slumped shoulders, slicked down black hair and pasty features belied the truth that he had more influence with the Democratic presidential candidate than any other liberal racketeer. He flicked ashes onto the freshly vacuumed beige carpet. "I can help you more by controlling the union and then move up to global oversight. We're already recruiting members from Europe and Asia."

Osama blew smoke toward the ceiling and grinned around his cigar. "You keep doing what you're doing and you can truly control the workers of the world."

Stylin got up and extended his hand which Osama stood up and shook with obvious appreciation. "That's exactly what I want," Stylin confided.

"Consider it done. We all set to meet with Georgie?"

"Yeah. See you at his place Sunday."

Youdi Mrderutu washed down prime rib with sparkling champagne and chuckled with amusement as he watched his cousin Barry Osama address an adoring crowd of low income voters in Youngstown, Ohio. Like Barry, Youdi was a radical Muslim with presidential aspirations in Kenya. He was three years older than Barry and mirrored the typical African demagogue.

"Change!! Barry shouted and glanced at his teleprompter. "Change from the failed Hush policies and the same old politics as usual. Change that will create jobs and security for you, the true backbone of this great nation. Change you can believe in.........change that will help you pay your mortgage and educate your children. Change that will force the fat cats to share America's wealth with you. Change in the way Washington does business. Change that will

transform the economy to provide future prosperity and

security." The crowd roared with approval and waved

banners denouncing the Hush administration and the war in

Iraq. Barry was the Messiah to lead them into a utopian

society.

Youdi had heard the same speech before. He and Barry

had teamed up and promised the Kenyans the change they

deserved. Youdi had perfected demagoguery during his

visits with Barry in the United States. Barry had sent his

foreign policy adviser to Kenya in 2006 to meet with

Muhammad Bloutomeca and Abduhl Behedu to pave the

way for Barry's summer visit to campaign for Youdi and

the Orange Democratic Movement.

Upon arrival in Kenya Barry had railed against the

"failed administrative policies of the current Kenyan

president" and echoed the "change" Youdi would bring to

government. Yeah! The horribly oppressed Kenyans

needed a charismatic and benevolent dictator to free them

from the peace and prosperity they enjoyed under a true

democratic government friendly with the United States.

Yes, indeed! Mrderutu, praised and supported by Osama,

promised to make Islam the only true religion of Kenya

and give Islamic leaders oversight of all other religions; to

install Shariah courts in every jurisdiction; to ban Christian

preaching; replacement of officials manipulated by

heathens and Zionists; adoption of a dress code for women

plus outlawing pork and gambling.

Barry, his father and Youdi were from the Luo tribe of

Muslims and Osama, Sr. was a devout communist who

taught that government is justified in taxing 100% of

personal income when providing services commensurate

with income taxed. Barry found it prudent to hide his

Islamic beliefs behind a Christian facade when pretending

to be a natural born American running for president.

The demagoguery foisted upon the Kenyan voters by Osama and Mrderutu did not sway enough votes and Youdi lost his bid for president of Kenya. Like any peace loving, generous, and gracious Muslim radical, Youdi and his followers resorted to terrorism to convince Kenyans of his good intentions. When you cannot get voted into office, just terrorize the folks until they give in to you in order to sleep peacefully.

So.....on the 2008 New Year day, a church full of Christians were locked inside the Assembly of God Church roughly 185 miles northwest of Nairobi in the village of Eldoret. The church was set ablaze and those who managed to get out were hacked to death with machetes by a mob of 2,000 Youdi disciples. Another 1,500 or so Kenyans were brutally murdered and a half million were displaced from their homes.

Perhaps Youdi learned the terrorists techniques as a communist student at East Germany's Magdeburg University in 1970 courtesy of the East German government. Although Youdi served eight years in prison for treason against the Kenyan government in 1982, Barry and Youdi promised the Kenyan people change and Youdi delivered it. If you make enough citizens afraid while hiding behind women and children it sometimes pays off. In 2008 Youdi Mrderutu was sworn in as Kenya's Prime Minister to quell the violence.

Youdi tinkled his golden bell to summon a houseboy to clear the table and pour more champagne. Barry was working the crowd to a frenzy of excitement. His political strategy had to be tailored to the laughable "rule of law" in the United States. The American people were not quite ready for a benevolent dictator. He had to get himself properly elected. Then he could sabotage capitalism and the free market; increase the number of citizens dependent

on government welfare from 45% to 52%; give more

illegal aliens the vote, appoint liberal radicals to the US

Supreme Court; weaken the military; and nudge the nation

into a world government dominated by Muslims.

Barry the Harvard graduate, polished orator,

accomplished liar and Muslim communist would also

eliminate personal incentives and redistribute the wealth of

America by taking from the rich and giving to the workers

of the world!

To pull off such deception Barry would stack his

administration with hard core socialists and communists.

Then, his cronies would be in charge of the nation's

treasury and could pilfer it at will since having total control

of both government and law enforcement placed them

firmly in the catbird seat. There would be nothing to stop

Barry's thugocracy from squirreling away billions.

CHAPTER TWO

Georgie Sorrow reclined with a snifter of very expensive brandy in his thickly padded chaise lounge chair and relished the possibilities presented by buying the White House for Barry Osama. Like King Solomon of Biblical fame, Georgie possessed peculiar treasures of every description from all over the world. Since he could have anything money could buy, material possessions did not drive his psychic energies.

He desperately wanted to lead mankind from capitalistic bondage to socialistic freedom. He loathed Walker and Linda Hush. He had almost succeeded in denying Hush a second term but the wars in Iraq and Afghanistan had kept him in the oval office.

But, Georgie had been successful in orchestrating an

economic crisis that Barry Osama could ride into the White House. Being a super rich radical liberal, Georgie had influenced the socialistic Democrats controlling Congress to coerce banks into real estate loans for low income citizens who didn't have a prayer of repaying the sub-prime mortgages when interest rates rebounded.

When Fannie Mae and Freddie Mack turned belly up along with most of the largest financial institutions in America, the economic disaster would be placed squarely on Hush's rounded shoulders. The Republican administration would be forced to take the heat for the Congressional idiocy.

The artificial housing bubble had actually been triggered under President Hinton's guidance although Billy and Lilly were too financially ignorant to understand the consequences of forcing the banks to make millions of bad loans to buy votes.

The value of real estate skyrocketed through supply and demand thereby creating an enormous and vastly inflated housing bubble which would blow up like a hydrogen bomb within the economy when millions of homeowners defaulted on loans they could not repay.

Real estate was accepted as reliable collateral for extending credit around the world. Yet, in the frenzy to pad portfolios and rake in huge commissions financial institutions issued mortgages to people with bad credit, no down payment and often no jobs.

Unfortunately, for President Hush and presidential candidate Jim McPaign the bubble burst in the fall of 2007 just as Georgie knew it would. The gullible public ignored the fact that liberal Democrats created the economic free fall and blamed Republicans egged on by the ultra liberal main stream media while shamelessly fawning over Osama. Without a doubt Georgie was going to have both

Congress and the White House helping him save the world from Republican incompetence.

Georgie was born in Hungary to a moderately wealthy Jewish couple on April 12, 1930. He was thirteen when the Nazi took control of his homeland and his father became a Nazi collaborator. Georgie was given protection at a handsome price by a Nazi official who presented him as his Christian godson. Georgie happily skipped along beside his bought father on his appointed rounds confiscating the property of Jews headed for the Nazi ovens. He would later say his conscience did not bother him because he was not the confiscator. He simply accompanied his Nazi godfather to avoid a terminal shower.

George Sorrow became a multi-billionaire without having any particular talent but the guts to take big risks in the stock market.....sort of like holding hands with the Nazis while his relatives were herded into death camps.

Georgie was now sixty-nine and wore his age well. He

stood at five feet, eight inches with a wiry frame and a

stern Jewish countenance. His slightly hooked nose, blue

eyes, rounded cheeks, and angular jawline marked him as

an American Jew. He conceived a unique twist in hedge

fund management and raked in billions when the British

sterling pound took an unprecedented dive in currency

trading. Working his way up the brokerage house ladder

had sharpened Georgie's instincts in sniffing out the most

unexpected shock waves within the capitalistic economies

where a Nazi educated Jew could strike it rich in one very

risky transaction.

The wealthier Georgie became, the more he hated

Republicans. He metamorphosed into a radical liberal and

donated heavily to socialistic agendas. Georgie coveted

nothing more than a major role in a world government

founded on socialism. Barry Osama would be his puppet

controlled by pulling the financial strings to foist him into

the American presidency. Like most egomaniacs Barry

would be easy to manipulate.

Jemama Osama had become a self-righteous racist

before puberty and nurtured her hatred of rich white

America through law school and into her brief legal career.

Why she surrendered her law license was never made

public and through Barry's political connections she

managed to land an executive position at Dumpew Medical

Center. Jemama and David Yurnany engineered a scheme

to collect taxpayer funding for poor uninsured patients.

The poor needing immediate medical care were

stabilized with the most expensive treatment options and

then dumped onto the street again to find cheaper longer

term care at other medical facilities accepting government

subsidies. Jemamacare was a sweet deal for Dumpew, and

Jemama recommended Yurnany's consulting service to

Senator Osama. Yurnany's natural knack for fleecing the

taxpayers and blaming the opposition appealed to Barry's

spirit of larceny.

Abdulla Tuckuen arrived for his 9:30 morning

appointment with the future First Lady and placed a heavy

envelope full of hundred dollar bills on her desk while she

poured his coffee and placed an apple fritter atop a linen

napkin.

"Busy morning?" Abdulla inquired.

"Yeah, my calendar's jammed. But I always got time for

you, my man. Looks like you made an early round and

picked some pockets." She smiled at the squat balding

Syrian who made and lost fortunes in real estate through

creative financing. Convicted of multiple fraudulent

transactions, Abdulla had spent some time being fed and

housed by Uncle Sam. One of his more recent schemes had

netted the Osamas close to half a million.

"A measly twenty grand but I got over a million in personal commitments. My business associates will cough it up when Barry needs a little boost." He nibbled at the fritter and sipped some steaming coffee. "You look mighty yummy this morning. Party must have ended early."

Jemama pretended to be flattered. She had long ago faced up to her lack of charm and eye appeal. She wore a perpetual scowl and didn't draw much attention from men. Her overly tall female frame was burdened with plump buttocks and wide hips. She wasn't really ugly, just less than attractive in a plain sort of way.

"Yeah. Fat cats can really be quite boring after a few drinks. Bless their liberal hearts. We need them more than they need us."

"Ain't that the god awful truth. I noticed the Dow took a dive when Heiny Takmore unveiled the Wall Street bailout.

Don't he and Hush live on the same planet? One might

suspect Heiny wants to bury the Republicans for the next

thirty years. Is he really that politically stupid?"

Jemama's scowl disappeared behind a cackling laugh.

"Would you trade your political allies for seven hundred

million? Heiny might be a lot of things, but dumb he ain't"

"I could make some new friends for that kinda bread."

Abdulla drained his cup, got up and straightened his bright

yellow tie. "Give Barry my regards. Gotta run to the bank

and tie up some loose ends."

Jeremiah Urmoni and Barry Osama were kindred spirits

creating racial disharmony for personal enrichment. They

were joined at the navels in 1988 when Barry was snorting

cocaine, perjuring himself to get financial aid, and

searching for a father figure to replace his Muslim

communist daddy who deserted him and his white hippie

mother along with another pregnant wife and infant son.

At age twenty-seven Barry adopted Urmoni as substitute father and spiritual mentor. Urmoni ministered to an Afrocentric church where he fleeced the congregation to build himself a million dollar home in a white gated community. Urmoni was pushing seventy, fragile build, wizened face, bald with a pencil mustache. The black racist pastor imprinted upon Barry his accusations that whites in America exploited and mightily oppressed Afro-American citizens and even invented AIDS to scourge folks of color.

White America catered to the blood sucking Jews who terrorized peaceful Palestinians by killing mostly women and children. The Zionist pigs robbed Palestinians of their homeland and reduced them to serfdom.

Moreover, the American warmongers nuked the peace loving Japanese and then cry about a handful of white Nazis killed in retribution by our Muslim brothers for terrorizing their homeland.

Yeah!! The chickens are coming home to roost. Damn America!! Damn the white bigots!! God damn America!! The government lies about everything. They lied in its founding documents. The American government purposely infected African-American men with syphilis.

Well, the people America has oppressed may not have great military might but they do have some individuals who are willing to die and take a few thousand with them. Yeah!! The chickens are indeed coming home to roost.

Barry Osama, the black knight from Mombosa, cousin to Youdi Mrderutu and accomplice in triggering the burning of Christians and murder of hundreds of his countrymen, listened to the racial ranting and vehement denouncement of America by Jeremiah Urmoni for twenty years and it just never occurred to Barry that Jeremiah might be a racist demagogue getting filthy rich off his enraptured Afro-American congregation.

That's what Barry told the media when Urmoni's sermons were reviewed by Telitright News. He just never thought of Jeremiah as a racial agitator. After all, Jeremiah married him and Jemama and baptized their two daughters. He was just like a father to him and he could not disavow him any more than he could his white grandmother who nearly fainted each time a black man passed her on the street. In denying the painfully obvious Barry practiced the same Rules For Radicals he taught to Forenborn Community Organizers recruits.

Barry Osama and Lilly Hinton, America's former First Lady, were devout Saul Alinsky students. Lilly softened her radicalism somewhat but Barry continued to practice and teach Alinsky's Rules for Radicals. Having been thoroughly brainwashed by Alinsky, his communist blood brothers Josif Givmeall, Jeremiah Urmoni, and Willie

Bombsetter; Barry's entire Ivy League education and brief

employment had been dedicated to teaching and practicing

deception to further socialist agendas.

Barry practiced what he preached and he taught

Forenborn recruits with religious fervor. Successful

revolutionaries act and dress professionally and infiltrate

the system from within. Converting capitalism into

socialism and ultimately communism is a slow and patient

process executed by penetrating universities, churches,

unions, and political parties by subterfuge and coalitions.

Slowly but surely the revolutionaries become a voting

majority to take control of a capitalistic democracy such as

the United States. Saul Alinsky's Rules for Radicals was

the bible from which Barry Osama conceived his political

ambitions. He was patient but persistent while working his

way from the bottom to the top of the unbelievably corrupt

Democratic monopoly in Chicago.

The infiltration process required two decades using carefully camouflaged radical organizations financed with hundreds of millions of taxpayer dollars. Barry had a true genius for milking the system and smelling the flowers along the way. He gradually became accepted by Chicago's political movers and shakers wining and dining each other while pilfering the public treasury. When it became strategically important to place another black homosexual advocate, abortionist and radical liberal from Illinois into the United States Senate, the Chicago politicians rallied around Barry Osama and sent him to Washington. From his seat in Congress, Barry Hussein Osama set his sights on the White House.

Willie Watchem thought about his guests for today's show and the Osama campaign. Teaching and practicing the most despicable, underhanded, and neatly camouflaged trickery imaginable, an African born Muslim communist

rode the gullibility of the American public all the way from

his birthplace in Mombosa, Kenya to become the

Democratic candidate for the presidency of the United

States. A monumental feat indeed made possible by strict

adherence to Saul Alinsky's masterpiece of subterfuge

foisted upon an apathetic population too occupied with self

indulgence to perceive the end of their personal freedom.

   To truly appreciate the insidious nature of the

acceleration of socialism and communistic ideology

steering the American way of life into oblivion, Watchem

mentally reviewed a sampling of what Barry Osama had

taught, believed and relied upon to "fundamentally

transform America." Osama was following to the letter

what Saul Alinsky had written in Rules For Radicals. He

thumbed through the book again:

          Opening page - Dedication

"Lest we forget at least an over-the-shoulder acknowledgment to the very first radical: from all our legends, mythology, and history... the first radical known to man who rebelled against the establishment and did it so effectively that he at least won his own kingdom — Lucifer"

Prologue

"The Revolutionary force today has two targets, moral as well as material. Its young protagonists are one moment reminiscent of the idealistic early Christians, yet they also urge violence and cry, 'Burn the system down!' They have no illusions about the system, but plenty of illusions about the way to change our world. It is to this point that I have written this book."

1. The Purpose

In this book we are concerned with how to create mass organizations to seize power and give it to the people; to realize the democratic dream of equality, justice, peace.... "Better to die on your feet than to live on your knees.' This means revolution." p.3

"Radicals must be resilient, adaptable to shifting political circumstances, and sensitive enough to the process of action and reaction to avoid being trapped by their own tactics and forced to travel a road not of their choosing." p.6

"A Marxist begins with his prime truth that all evils are caused by the exploitation of the proletariat by the capitalists. From this he logically proceeds to the revolution to end capitalism, then into the third stage of

reorganization into a new social order of the

dictatorship of the proletariat, and finally the

last stage -- the political paradise of

communism." p.10

"An organizer working in and for an open

society is in an ideological dilemma to begin

with, he does not have a fixed truth -- truth to

him is relative and changing; everything to him

is relative and changing.... To the extent that he

is free from the shackles of dogma, he can

respond to the realities of the widely different

situations...." pp.10-11

  2. Of Means and Ends   [Forget moral or

ethical considerations]

"The end is what you want, the means is how

you get it. Whenever we think about social

change, the question of means and ends arises.

The man of action views the issue of means

and ends in pragmatic and strategic terms. He

has no other problem; he thinks only of his

actual resources and the possibilities of various

choices of action. He asks of ends only whether

they are achievable and worth the cost; of

means, only whether they will work. ... The

real arena is corrupt and bloody." p.24

"The means-and-ends moralists, constantly

obsessed with the ethics of the means used by

the Have-Nots against the Haves, should search

themselves as to their real political position. In

fact, they are passive — but real — allies of the

Haves.... The most unethical of all means is

the non-use of any means... The standards of

judgment must be rooted in the whys and

wherefores of life as it is lived, the world as it

is, not our wished-for fantasy of the world as it

should be...." pp.25-26

"The third rule of ethics of means and ends is

that in war the end justifies almost any

means...." p.29

"The seventh rule... is that generally success or

failure is a mighty determinant of ethics...."

p.34

"The tenth rule... is you do what you can with

what you have and clothe it with moral

garments.... It involves sifting the multiple

factors which combine in creating the

circumstances at any given time... Who, and

how many will support the action?... If

weapons are needed, then are appropriate

weapons available? Availability of means

determines whether you will be underground or

above ground; whether you will move quickly

or slowly..." p.36

4. The Education of the Organizer

"To the organizer, imagination... is the

dynamism that starts and sustains him in his

whole life of action as an organizer. It ignites

and feeds the force that drives him to organize

for change....

"The organizer knows that the real action is in

the reaction of the opposition. To realistically

appraise and anticipate the probable reactions

of the enemy, he must be able to identify with

them, too, in his imagination, and foresee their

reactions to his actions....

"The organizers searching with a free and open mind void of certainty, hating dogma, finds laughter not just a way to maintain his sanity but also a key to understanding life."pp.74-75

"...the organizer must be able to split himself into two parts -- one part in the arena of action where he polarizes the issue to 100 to nothing, and helps to lead his forces into conflict, while the other part knows that when the time comes for negotiations that it really is only a 10 percent difference." p.78

"...the organizer is constantly creating new out of the old. He knows that all new ideas arise from conflict; [See Dialectic Process] that every time man as had a new idea it has been a challenge to the sacred ideas of the past and the present and inevitably a conflict has raged."

p.79

5. Communication   [Notice the emphasis on

conflict, dialogue, relationships, etc. Team

"service" is essential to building strong

relationships through "common involvements"]

"And so the guided questioning goes on

without anyone losing face or being left out of

the decision-making. Every weakness of every

proposed tactic is probed by questions.... Is this

manipulation? Certainly...." p.88

"One of the factors that changes what you can

and can't communicate is relationships. There

are sensitive areas that one does not touch until

there is a strong personal relationship based on

common involvements. Otherwise the other

party turns off and literally does not hear....

"Conversely, if you have a good relationship,

he is very receptive.... For example, I have

always believed that birth control and abortion

are personal rights to be exercised by the

individual. If, in my early days when I

organized... neighborhood in Chicago, which

was 95 per cent Roman Catholic, I had tried to

communicate this, even through the experience

of the residents, whose economic plight was

aggravated by large families, that would have

been the end of my relationship with the

community. That instant I would have been

stamped as an enemy of the church and all

communication would have ceased.

"Some years later, after establishing solid

relationships, I was free to talk about

anything.... By then the argument was no

longer limited to such questions as, 'How much

longer do you think the Catholic Church can

hang on to this archaic notion and still survive?'

...the subject and nature of the discussion

would have been unthinkable without that solid

relationship." pp.93-94

6. In the Beginning: The Process of Power

[Notice the compromise needed to build the

power base. Yet, since pragmatism has eroded

all values, it's simply a matter of ends justifying

means. It's not unlike churches that attract

members through the world's entertainment --

then continue to soften or hide Truth in order to

keep them happy and lure more.]

"From the moment the organizer enters a

community he lives, dreams... only one thing

and that is to build the mass power base of

what he calls the army. Until he has developed

that mass power base, he confronts no major

issues.... Until he has those means and power

instruments, his 'tactics' are very different from

power tactics. Therefore, every move revolves

around one central point: how many recruits

will this bring into the organization, whether by

means of local organizations, churches, service

groups, labor Unions, corner gangs, or as

individuals."

"Change comes from power, and power comes

from organization." p.113

"The first step in community organization is

community disorganization. The disruption of

the present organization is the first step toward

community organization. Present arrangements

must be disorganized if they are to be displace

by new patterns.... All change means

disorganization of the old and organization of

the new." p.116

"An organizer must stir up dissatisfaction and

discontent... He must create a mechanism that

can drain off the underlying guilt for having

accepted the previous situation for so long a

time. Out of this mechanism, a new community

organization arises....

"The job then is getting the people to move, to

act, to participate; in short, to develop and

harness the necessary power to effectively

conflict with the prevailing patterns and change

them. When those prominent in the status quo

turn and label you an 'agitator' they are

completely correct, for that is, in one word,

your function—to agitate to the point of

conflict." p.117

"Process tells us how. Purpose tells us why. But in reality, it is academic to draw a line between them, they are part of a continuum.... Process is really purpose." p.122

7. Tactics

"Tactics are those conscious deliberate acts by which human beings live with each other and deal with the world around them. ... Here our concern is with the tactic of taking; how the Have-Nots can take power away from the Haves." p.126

Always remember the first rule of power tactics (pps.127-134):

1. "Power is not only what you have, but what the enemy thinks you have."

2. "Never go outside the expertise of your people. When an action or tactic is outside the experience of the people, the result is confusion, fear and retreat.... [and] the collapse of communication.

3. "Whenever possible, go outside the expertise of the enemy. Look for ways to increase insecurity, anxiety and uncertainty. (This happens all the time. Watch how many organizations under attack are blind-sided by seemingly irrelevant arguments that they are then forced to address.)

4. "Make the enemy live up to its own book of rules. You can kill them with this, for they can no more obey their own rules than the Christian church can live up to Christianity."

5. "Ridicule is man's most potent weapon. It is almost impossible to counteract ridicule. Also it infuriates the opposition, which then reacts to your advantage."

6. "A good tactic is one your people enjoy."

7. "A tactic that drags on too long becomes a drag. Man can sustain militant interest in any issue for only a limited time...."

8. "Keep the pressure on, with different tactics and actions, and utilize all events of the period for your purpose."

9. "The threat is usually more terrifying than the thing itself."

10. "The major premise for tactics is the development of operations that will maintain a

constant pressure upon the opposition. It is this unceasing pressure that results in the reactions from the opposition that are essential for the success of the campaign."

11. "If you push a negative hard and deep enough, it will break through into its counter side... every positive has its negative."

12. "The price of a successful attack is a constructive alternative."

13. Pick the target, freeze it, personalize it, and polarize it. In conflict tactics there are certain rules that [should be regarded] as universalities. One is that the opposition must be singled out as the target and 'frozen.'...

Barry Osama impressed upon Forenborn's recruits

that "you do what you can with what you have and clothe it with moral arguments. Moral rationalization is indispensable at all times of action whether to justify the selection or the use of ends or means. Raise questions that agitate and break through the accepted norm. Nothing is sacred. The effective organizer detests dogma and any definition of morality. The most potent weapons known to mankind are satire and ridicule delivered with a sense of humor. The organizer's first task is to create the issues of problems; rub raw the resentments of the people; fan the latent hostilities; search out controversy and stir up dissatisfaction and discontent."

For half a century liberal revolutionaries like Barry Hussein Osama have cleverly and conscientiously undermined the Christian morality upon which America was founded and skyrocketed to the most powerful and

wealthiest nation on Earth. The United States gross

national product (GNP) represents approximately one

fourth of the world's combined GNP. The United States

military is unparalleled in the history of humanity and the

standard of living including healthcare is unmatched by

any other nation.

But, the Barry Osamas among us are

determined to convert American citizens to

government wards to be equally fed, clothed

and housed at the expense of individual liberty.

The wealthy spawned by personal creativity

and productivity must be brought down to the

same level as the those willingly uneducated,

lazy and producing offspring they cannot feed.

To realize the liberal utopia where all share

equally, the first task had been to eliminate all

family values; ridicule all morality and
embrace blasphemy, infanticide and
homosexuality. Homosexual romance was
taught to kindergarten children. Teenagers were
encouraged to sodomize each other. Sexual
perverts were sent to Congress. Homosexual,
evolution spouting, abortionists were appointed
to the federal bench.

Children were taught that America is an evil
country that oppresses the poor and
underprivileged. Students were graduated from
high school who cannot read a bus schedule.
American history was rewritten as the home of
capitalistic pigs and bigoted religious fanatics.
The Bible had to be forbidden reading. The
Christian God had to be reduced to a form of
profanity and Islam viewed as a peaceful and

virtuous form of worship where suicide

bombers were ushered directly into paradise to

copulate eternally with seventy-two brown

eyed virgins.

Apathetic Christians must vote to be

governed by a proponent of abortion, anti-

Christ teachings, sexual perversion and

communist ideology in exchange for a five

hundred dollar government check.

Homosexuals must be revered in Christian

churches and ordained into the Christian

ministry. The United States must

metamorphose into a 21st century Sodom and

Gomorrah bent upon committing national

suicide by merging into a one world

government where all citizens can be equally

poor and underprivileged.   Watchem laid aside

the book and reviewed his notes for each guest.

He would ask the hard questions and let his

viewers judge the answers.

CHAPTER THREE

Sambo Mellon, Jerry Jerkman, and Allan Snowyew

appeared somewhat nervous and a little apprehensive as

Willie Watchem, talk show host at Telitright News,

welcomed them to the show with a brief introduction of

each guest. Willie resonated with charm and intelligence.

He was a handsome, green-eyed, brown headed six footer

with muscular frame, flashing white teeth and disarming

smile. His voice was clear and pleasant:

"Our distinguished guests tonight are Jerry

Jerkman, Executive Editor for Weeklynews;

Sambo Mellon, Executive Vice President at

Forenborn Community Organizers; Allan

Snowyew, Nobel Prize recipient for his

personal commitment to save the planet from

global warming; and Rivera Kildajew, talk

show host and part-time investigative reporter.

Welcome Gentlemen, and thank you for

appearing on the show. My first question is for

Sambo: I understand that the Attorney

Generals of six states are investigating

Forenborn for several counts of election fraud.

Is this fact or fiction?"

Sambo wrinkled his black forehead and

coughed to give himself a second or two to

think up a response. He was dressed in subdued

business attire and reflected the image of a

clean cut middle-aged executive with gray

flecked hair and cultured education.

"Well, actually a little of both. Forenborn is

being investigated in several states but the

accusations are pure fiction. We are doing what

we always do........help folks in low income

neighborhoods get registered to vote. You

know.....ah....ah help them fill out forms, get to

the registration facility, and encourage them to

familiarize themselves with the issues that

affect their daily lives."

Watchem shuffled through a stack of notes

and looked into Sambo's eyes without blinking.

"That's very commendable. But I'm a little

confused by your registration assistance. How

many times do you help the same person

register to vote?"

Sambo pretended surprise at the question.

"It's illegal to register more than once.

Sometimes, when someone messes up a form,

we help them fill out a new one. We often help

folks who have difficulty deciphering legal

forms."

Jerkman and Allan nodded understandingly.

Watchem looked blandly at Sambo. "You mean

conscientious voters who never bothered to

educate themselves enough to read and write?"

Sambo's tone became defensive. "You must

consider that the people we assist are greatly

oppressed and forced to live in ghettos run by

slumlords. They are denied a proper education

by the capitalistic system which keeps them

subservient and attending inferior schools."

"Are you saying that our mandatory

education for all children and trillions of

welfare dollars is not adequate to teach children

from low income neighborhoods the

fundamentals of reading, writing and

arithmetic? And, don't we bus kids from your

so called ghettos whose parents pay nothing to

support public schools to middle class white

neighborhood schools and bus white kids to

schools in predominantly black

neighborhoods?"

Sambo feigned a disgusted response.

"Superficial integration of public schools is just

a sham to avoid addressing the psychic needs

of black children subjected to the hatred and

bigotry of white America. We need a

transformation in this country to give all our

citizens an equal opportunity to acquire a

proper education and become productive

members of society."

Watchem looked puzzled. "Didn't we pass

equal opportunity laws over forty years ago?

And, don't we have Afro-Americans who took

advantage of such equal opportunity prospering

as lawyers, doctors, professors, businessmen,

multimillionaire professional athletes, members

of Congress, and isn't one of the richest

individuals in America a black woman; and

isn't a black man running for president of these

United States. What can we do for those who

choose to willingly remain uneducated, refuse

to work, and keep making babies for others to

feed, clothe and shelter. What more do your

poor and underprivileged welfare sponges

need? Perhaps to be spoon fed so they don't

have to exercise their elbows to eat?"

Sambo's eyes pleaded with Jerkman and Allan for a little

support.

"Afro-American are treated as second class citizens and denied the dignity and self-respect to which they are entitled as fellow citizens. At Forenborn we are doing what we can to combat bigotry and hatred."

Watchem displayed irritation with Sambo's racist rhetoric. "That is a tired and offensive community organizer byline to convince those on the public dole that they need Forenborn to defend their civil rights which every American I know already respects and defends. Watchem smiled with controlled contempt and punched a button on his electronic menu console. A white viewing screen descended noiselessly down the opposite wall in perfect position to be viewed by both Watchem and his three guests.

"Let's move on shall we from oppressing folks of color to helping them register to vote. These interviews were conducted yesterday in Cleveland, Ohio. We'll just listen

and let the people themselves explain your necessary

assistance in filling out those complex, confusing legal

forms."

On the screen a very attractive blonde researcher

extended a portable microphone toward a rotund middle-

aged black lady posing for the camera.

"Do you mind if I ask your name?"

"Oh, it ain't no secret. I'm Rowanda White. "

"Is Tuesday your day off?

"I don't got no day off. I gots seven kids to look after.

Ain't got time for no job. Just cooking, cleaning, and

babysittin' chores."

"Is your husband employed?"

"Ain't got no husband but I gots men friends now and

then."

"Are you registering to vote?"

Rowanda smiled sheepishly. "I been doing that all this week and helpin' out them Forenborn workers."

The researcher looked confused. "Helping Forenborn? I don't understand."

"I'se helpin' them nice fellas with their commissions. Theys git paid on how many cards theys turn in and I gets twenty dollars for each card I fills out for 'em."

"How many cards have you filled out?"

"Bout 70 I guess. Ain't no bother. Just fills out the name n' address and check some boxes. Ain't much to it and it pays real good"

"So you made fourteen hundred dollars so far helping Forenborn out?"

"Sounds bout right. I kin sure use the extra money. Bout outta food stamps and I don't gits my welfare check til next Friday."

"Do you use a different name and address for each card

you fill out?"

"Yessum. Dey give me the name n' address and I does the rest."

"Why do you think Forenborn needs all those registrations?"

"Dey tells me I'm filling out cards for dem who wanna vote but can't read n' write soes I just helpin' out."

"Thank you, Rowanda. You've been a big help."

"No bother atall. Nice talkin' wid you."

The researcher rolled her eyes at her cameraman and shook her head in stunned wonderment.

The screen darkened and then lit up again. The same researcher is shown chatting with an elderly man wearing a Cleveland Indians baseball cap and carrying a bottle wrapped in a brown paper sack.

"Indians looked pretty good for a while, then folded. What happened?"

"Shore did. Our pitchin' fell apart. We git 'em next year."

"If you don't mind me asking, Roy, are you registered to vote?"

"Shore nuff. Gots to vote fo my man Barry."

"Ms. White down the block tells me she's helping out Forenborn with getting folks in the neighborhood registered to vote. Has Forenborn asked you to help?"

"Yep. I'm helpin' all I kin. Shore is a lotta people who needs help fillin' out them registration cards who wanna vote but can't write."

"So, you're helping by filling out cards for some of these people?"

"Done filled out sixty-seven. Easy to do. Don't take much effort and I gets paid mor'en I should. But, I ain't complaining."

"Are a lot of your neighbors helping out too?"

"Bout everybody I knows. We all helpin' out."

The researcher shook Roy's hand. "I appreciate you chatting with me."

Willie Watchem flipped the control button off and glanced around at each guest.

"Well, I assume that clears up those unfounded charges of election fraud on the part of Forenborn. Just another day looking after the poor and underprivileged on the streets of a swing state."

Sambo, Jerkman and Allan struggled to maintain their composure. Sambo looked up at the ceiling.

"We'll weed out those street workers padding commissions and put in controls to eliminate any further irregularities. I'm confident that these are isolated incidents of misconduct."

"Misconduct?" Watchem quizzed. "Looks pretty well planned to me." He switched his focus to Jerry Jerkman.

"I noted with some puzzlement that Weeklynews

obviously did not think that Barry Osama's long time and

close personal relationship with a confessed domestic

terrorist, an avowed communist, a real estate con artist and

a Kenyan mass murderer is newsworthy. Can you explain

why Weeklynews came to that conclusion?"

Jerkman was sixty-four, obese with sagging cheeks,

gray eyes, wrinkled forehead, stained dentures and pointed

chin. He folded his hands over his chest with an editor's

smirk.

"Willie Bombsetter is nothing more than one of Barry's

neighbors by happenstance. Barry hadn't reached puberty

when Willie was behaving as a domestic terrorist. Willie

was acquitted at trial and is now a respected university

professor. Communists are just another political party

enjoying freedom of speech in America. Abdulla Tuckuen

has certainly sold real estate to a lot of people other than the Osamas. We, at Weeklynews, do not hold Barry

responsible for what some rebel does in Africa."

Watchem finished jotting down his notes and looked

over at Jerkman. "Weeklynews doesn't hold Barry Osama

responsible for anything whatsoever. Like not producing an

official birth certificate and admitting himself to be foreign

born when applying for financial aid; flying on a foreign

passport to Pakistan when it was illegal for Americans to

do so; or helping his Muslim cousin stage terrorism,

murder and mayhem in Osama's home country of Kenya;

taking part in a fraudulent real estate scheme that netted

him an illegal half million dollars; or denying statements

by his paternal grandmother and Kenyan Ambassador that

he was born in Mombosa, Kenya; or intimate relationships

with ex-convicts, tax cheats, socialists, communists, and

Muslim radicals; selecting a known terrorist, murderer,

and treasonous left wing radical to ghostwrite his

biography and launch his political career by throwing a

party for communist friends to raise initial campaign

funds." Willie smiled pleasantly when Jerkman looked

rattled.

"I would postulate Mr. Jerkman that Willie Bombsetter

was and is more than just an innocent neighbor; that Osama

allegedly being a Harvard graduate knew that his real

estate deal with Tuckuen was both fraudulent and a felony

crime; that Osama was a willing accomplice to terrorism,

murder and mayhem in Kenya by providing the support of

his senate seat in Congress to a cold blooded killer and

close relative; that Osama is an imposter, criminal, and a

foreign born Muslim radical foisting himself upon

politically ignorant voters more interested in government

handouts than where Osama was born and who he

associates with. Apparently, Barry Hussein Osama was

thrown down to us from the gods. No one at Harvard

remembers him. He cannot produce a valid United States

birth certificate. He refuses to produce any scholastic

records or any academic awards. We know nothing about

his education other than his own self-serving statements.

He has never owned, directed or managed any type of

enterprise. He has zero foreign relations experience. He is

totally ignorant of fundamental economics. His political

views are blatantly racist and he openly refers to Muslim

terrorists as his brothers. He has repeatedly proven himself

to be a liar, con man, racial agitator and communist at

heart. Why don't you challenge me on these statements, Mr.

Jerkman?"

Watchem turned in his swivel chair to face Allan

Snowyew. "Allen, it is snowing in the desert. Our

northern states are iced in. Global temperatures have been

cooling for at least a decade. Polar bear populations are

increasing. Scientists have been manipulating and

fabricating statistical data to support global warming when in fact the opposite is occurring. Do you have some credible data to share with us?"

Allan Snowyew laced his fingers and tapped his thumbs. He sported a thick shock of light brown hair freshly barbered, a roman nose, high cheek bones, smooth pale complexion, hazel eyes, square jaws and stout chin. He was a former Vice President of the United States and claimed to have invented the internet. He was becoming a multimillionaire over and above his inherited fortune by exploiting public ignorance of climatology. Allan knew that the general American public could not read scientific data let alone understand the symbols and formulas. Only one in four Americans earned a college degree and less than five percent matriculated in Earth Science. Nevertheless, Allan knew full well that Willie Watchem read and understood climatology text books. After observing the pummeling

Sambo endured, he would be very careful in fielding

Watchem's questions. He leaned back in a relaxed position.

"The more recent studies do show an interim cooling

trend but the hard data compiled over the last century

indicates that we are gradually destroying the ozone layer

that protects Earth from cosmic radiation which will in fact

melt the polar ice caps and raise ocean levels causing

extensive environmental damage and quite possibly human

extinction." Allan conjured up a concerned frown. "We

simply must adopt non-polluting energy sources and each

of us take personal responsibility for protecting our

severely damaged planet."

"How about you, Allan. Do you take personal

responsibility for protecting planet Earth?" Watchem

suppressed a laugh as Allan's cheeks reddened.

"Yes, I do. I take my personal responsibility very

seriously."

"Even when you eat all those steaks you love carved from butchered cows that pass methane into the air and eat corn and hay produced by farm machinery puffing out carbon dioxide?"

"All of us must sacrifice by converting to vegetarians to reduce the carbon dioxide pollution caused by breeding and feeding livestock including cattle, hogs, sheep, goats, and chickens. I intend to make that conversion in the near future."

"Did you get here today by walking or by bicycle; or did you arrive in a motor vehicle spewing harmful fumes into our atmosphere?"

Allan squirmed in his chair. "My schedule is very hectic so I came by taxi to avoid being late. Otherwise, I would have taken the electric subway."

"Oh, I see," Willie said in a sympathetic voice. "Your business activities and personal comfort are more important than protecting the environment. I guess that

holds true for the jet planes you travel around in and for the

energy consumption at your personal residence where you

use twelve times the dirty energy used by the average

American household?"

Allan appeared more and more uncomfortable. "I'm

having energy saving devices installed in my home and I

only use air travel because I currently have no other option

available to accommodate my global travels."

Willie eyed Allan blandly. "You could just not travel and

thus demonstrate that you take your personal responsibility

seriously to protect the planet and prolong our survival as

non-polluters. You could leave early for local appointments

and walk or ride a bike. You could turn off your furnace

and wear coats over sweaters to keep warm. You could turn

off three out of every four lights in your home, all the

outside lights and stop watching TV. You could shut off

your hot water heater and shower and shave using cold

water. That is, if you are really serious about doing your

part to save the planet."

Allan turned defensive. "I have never recommended

such drastic changes in our lifestyle. There is much that

can be accomplished by developing clean energy without

sacrificing personal comfort."

Willie Watchem went for the jugular. "Are you a

climatologist Allan?"

"No, but I have studied global warming extensively and

know that carbon dioxide emissions must be sharply

reduced or we human beings face certain extinction."

Watchem chuckled with disdain. "Nothing could be

further from the truth, Allan. According to Dr. S. Fred

Singer, atmospheric physicist and Professor Emeritus of

Environmental Sciences at the University of Virginia and

former director of the US Weather Satellite Service, if

every nation on Earth complied with the current pledged

reductions in atmospheric gases contributing to global

warming, the effect on future temperatures would be of no

consequence whatsoever; perhaps one twentieth of one

degree by the year 2050."

"I'm not familiar with that report," Allan said testily.

"How about this one, Allan. Dr. Wallace Broecker, a

leading world authority on climate, Lamont-Doherty Earth

Observatory, Columbia University, said in a 1996 speech in

Baltimore, Maryland: 'I can only see one element of the

climate system capable of generating these fast, global

changes, that is, changes in the tropical atmosphere leading

to changes in the inventory of the earth's most powerful

greenhouse gas --- water vapor.'

Now, Allan, water vapor only contains one thousandth of

one percent man-made gases and contributes to 95% of the

total greenhouse effect while carbon dioxide plus methane

contribute only 3.978%; nitrous oxide .0950% and all other anthropogenic gases .072%. What these numbers prove is that if we humans discontinued all farming, manufacturing, energy production and transportation activities, the impact on global warming would be negligible for the foreseeable future."

Allan knew he had been exposed on national TV as a con artist. "I can quote you numerous studies that prove precisely the opposite."

"No, you cannot Allan. What you can show me are biased reports of studies where the goal is to get more taxpayer money for more biased research to get more taxpayer money. All of these phony research studies intentionally do not include the impact of water vapor on the greenhouse effect and man has virtually zero impact on global water vapor. Global warming protests give rich kids a cause to champion to relieve pure boredom and give con artists and former Vice Presidents a drum to beat on the talk show circuit. You're getting filthy rich, Allan, off public ignorance pertaining to Earth science."

Allan started to throw out more cliches but was preempted by a Viagra commercial. When the commercial ended, Willie turned his attention to Rivera Kildajew who looked a wee bit apprehensive after watching his fellow guests take it on the chin. Rivera sported a stiff handlebar mustache framing teeth too big for his mouth. He squinted at Willie through bifocal lenses and brushed some lint off his checkered sweater draped over his flannel shirt and baggy jeans. Rivera fancied himself as a bold "ladies man" and appeared to believe that all of Willie's audience waited with bated breath to hear his wisdom and wit. He brushed back his rust colored long hair dangling over his pierced ears while flashing a toothy smile at Willie.

"Saved me for last, did ya. Well, Willie Boy, bring it

on!" Willie chuckled, reached over and shook Rivera's

hand with feigned appreciation. "Always a pleasure to chat

with you and hear your latest exploits. Just a couple of

quick questions for you as my air time is fading fast. I

heard your comments on the recent Israeli war crimes and I

just want to check with you and make sure I got the true

facts covering what is really happening. As I understand

the fast moving events, Hamas fired more than a thousand

rockets into Israel while hiding their launching equipment

and operations next to schools, hospitals, and other civilian

facilities so as to use the Palestinians who voted them into

power as human shields. The geographical areas used by

Hamas to force Palestinians to face incoming Israeli

retaliatory fire aimed at halting the unprovoked Hamas

rocket attacks are part and parcel of a demilitarized zone as

established by an agreement between Israel and the

Palestinians. Consequently, Hamas not only broke the truce

agreements, but hid weapons and launch pads behind

women and children while firing thousands of rockets

indiscriminately into Israeli cities without any provocation

whatsoever. Hamas planned to randomly murder as many

Israeli women and children as humanly possible and then

accuse Israel of war crimes and inhuman waging of war

when some of the civilians Hamas is hiding behind get

killed by incoming Israeli fire aimed at stopping the

incoming Hamas rockets. How am I doing so far, Mr.

Kildajew? Did I get it right?"

Rivera did his famous "eyebrows to the ceiling look"

and folded his hands in front of his doughy belly. "The

Jews and Arabs have been fighting over a few acres in the

Middle East forever. The Jews have consistently

confiscated Arab land and tossed the Arab civilians into the

gutters. A few terrorists grew tired of Zionist illegal

occupation and shot a few rockets into Israel to draw

attention to the confiscation of their land. Israel used jet

fighters and state of the art artillery to kill off Palestinian

women and children to the tune of 29 for every Israeli

soldier killed during the heroic defense by Hamas. Yes. I

would think that qualifies as war crimes."

Willie stared at Rivera in total amazement. "Mr.

Kildajew. You are surely named in accordance with your

blind bias and are talking like a Hamas terrorist with total

disregard for reality. Where were you in 1948 when the

British caved in to the United Nations and established a

tiny homeland for Jews escaping genocide in Europe. The

homeland mandate for Jews covered a tiny geographical

area about the size of our state of New Jersey where Jews

had been living under persecution and oppression for more

than 2,500 years. The homeland mandated was basically

little more than a desert with no agriculture exporting, no

economy to speak of, and no modern transportation,

sewage, drinkable water supply or communications

network. Half a dozen or so Arab nations armed with

modern weapons gifted by the British attacked the Israeli

refugees who were armed with nothing but rifles,

handguns, knives, and a lot of guts. Only interference by

Western nations saved the Arab mad dogs from

extermination by the Jewish refugees. You know, Mr.

Kildajew, kind of like the Texas Alamo in reverse. Whatta

you think? Should we give Texas to Mexican drug lords if

they fire a few thousand Iranian rockets into Houston and

Dallas? How about our thirteen colonies which grew into

the United States of America. We were attacked by the

British and won the war we waged form our freedom. Shall

we abandon the US and turn it over to England if a few

rag-headed terrorists living in England fire a few thousand

Iranian and Russian missiles into Boston and Philadelphia

killing a bunch of American women and children? How

big a flaming hypocrite and Muslim propaganda artist are

you? You wanna truly talk "disproportionate retaliation

against mad dog enemies?" How about the dozen or so

men dropping the atomic bomb on Japanese cities killing

hundreds of thousands of civilians while eliminating some

military facilities? Might that qualify as disproportionate?

Of course, the Japanese attacked Pearl Harbor during a

time of peace killing a few thousand of our sailors; hacked

the arms and legs off American POW's and refused to

surrender after losing the war which prompted us to use the

atomic bomb to change their mind. Wake up Mr. Kildajew!

The Arab terrorists openly scream for the total destruction

of Israel and confiscation of all Israeli land and property.

The Jews are simply saying that is not going to happen

although you force us to kill you and your civilian

population who allow you to hide behind them and fire

rockets into Israel hoping to kill our women and children.

So, go ahead, your big, mean, loudmouthed terrorist scum. You attack us and we will defend ourselves. If you hide behind your women and children some of them are going to get killed just as you hope so that you can go crying to the world about how heartless we Israelis are in fending off your terrorist attacks." What say you, Mr. Kildajew? Does that sound like war in the twenty-first century?"

Rivera shook his head sadly. "The Jews do not have to kill the Palestinians. Just give them their own State and live together peacefully." Willie laughed out loud. "Why, sure!!! Nothing to it. Just let the terrorists set up a permanent armed camp inside Israeli borders so they don't have to pay Iran for those long range rockets. The short range ones will work just fine when firing across the city limits."

Willie eyed Kildajew with disdain. "How about the '67 war' when Arabs again got very brave by combining their armies and weapons to kill Israeli women and children?

They don't want to fight the Israeli army because they

consistently get their asses kicked. They prefer to target

Israeli women and children and then cry like spoiled babies

when the human shields they hide behind catch some

Israeli artillery fire or get bombed along with Hama

weapons. Wake up! If you love terrorists so much, take a

fast train from the land of the free and the home of the

brave to Gaza and let Hamas use you to shield their rocket

launchers. I find it most interesting that the Palestinians did

not decide the land belonged to them until after the Israelis

converted the desert into a productive 'cash cow garden.'

Now that California grows a lot of produce and earns

billions, do you actually believe we should give the state to

thugs who claim they homesteaded California?"

Willie forced himself to smile graciously. "Lets talk a

couple of minutes about gun control legislation. Why did

the framers of our constitution guarantee all Americans the

right to carry arms? Was it to hunt for meat or to protect

American citizens from the type of government Barry

Osama envisions for this nation?

Rivera adopted the Jessie Jackman ministerial scowl.

"We must pass more strict gun control legislation to keep

mental cases from gunning down innocent civilians going

about their lives at school, at work, at church, at home and

performing public service."

Willie now looked like a man who owned a few guns.

His tone bordered on contempt. "Why are the radical

liberals always seeking new arguments for the government

to take our guns? The absolute truth is so that only the

government has legal guns and can kill us at the whim of

some dictatorial power mad and oily politician like Barry

Osama backed up by his criminal administration. Criminals

will find a way to get guns. Gun control only takes the

guns out of the hands of law abiding citizens. The framers

of our federal constitution guaranteed American citizens

the right to bear arms to be able to resist government

tyranny. If the Osamas of our generation get our guns, a lot

of American citizens are going to be murdered as political

opponents. Who, in their right mind would attempt to

subjugate 160 to 170 million armed citizens even if the

military leaders appointed by our "dead of the night"

sneaky, underhanded Congress and communist president

work hand in hand to kill the hard core opposition and

imprison millions more in FEMA concentration camps.

The camps now exist and are ready for a resistance

population. It has happened several times before during the

last century where the citizenship was unarmed. Osama,

the Supreme Court, Congress and federal judges have

already shredded our constitution and rewrote it from the

bench to suit the radical liberal agenda. Gun control based

on the fact that some crazed idiots use guns to kill innocent

people is moronic and self-serving to those who want to

subjugate us. I heard recently that some mental midget

fatally stabbed an elderly man who was minding his own

business. AHA!!!! Let's outlaw knives in the hands of our

citizens to stop such killings. How about where a husband

choked his wife, Should we cut off everyone's hands so

nobody gets choked? Or maybe we should strip our

citizens of electric lamps because a wife based her

husband's head in with a desk lamp. Guns in the hands of

law abiding citizens do not kill people. People kill people

using knives, rocks, ball bats, hatchets, axes, meat cleavers,

ice picks, screwdrivers, and, yes, guns. However, honest,

law abiding citizens need guns to protect their homeland

against military coups, would-be dictators, and power mad

people like Georgie Sorrow who funded Osama's sneaking

into the White House by a cool billion dollars. If

Americans did not have the right to bear arms, there would

be no United States because there would have been no

Revolutionary War led by American colonists. No, Mr.

Kildajew. I am not surrendering my legal, constitution-ally

protected guns. And, King Osama better not try to take

them. There will be a lot of dead thugs found on my

property."

Rivera squinted at Willie. "Isn't that a bit extreme?"

Willie lost all tolerance for Kildajew's stupidity. "It

depends upon whether you're doing the killing or being

killed. How many people, in fact, have been killed by

government violence in the 20th century? Not deaths in

wars and civil wars among military combatants, but mass

murder of civilians and innocent victims with either the

approval or planning of governments — the intentional

killings of their own subjects and citizens or people under

their political control? The answer is: 169,198,000. If the

deaths of military combatants are added to this figure,

governments have killed 203,000,000 in the 20th century.

The world population in 1991 is estimated to have been

approximately 5,423,000,000. In 1991, Europe's population

was about 502,000,000. The United States in 1990 had a

population of about 249,000,000. This means that

governments killed about 3.7 percent of the human race in

this century, or an equivalent of over 40 percent of all the

people in Europe, or a number equal to over 80 percent of

all the people in the U.S.

Willie smiled tightly into the main camera. "Sorry

folks. This show was just beginning to be worth watching.

But, we are out of time and must move on to the Bill

Smiley Show. I understand that Lilly Hinton is going to

convince Bill to vote for her. Good, luck, Lilly."

Lilly Hinton coveted the feminist and abortionist votes. Personally, she could care less whether mommies should or should not kill babies in the womb. What Lilly wanted was to be President of the United States. Former president, Billy Hinton, had proven to her that the most outrageous deeds would be overlooked by the American voters if defended with style and described candidly.

Thus, Lilly was confident as she faced Bill Smiley on Telitright News Gottcha talk show. She wore a pale blue ladies business suit with no jewelry other than her wedding band. She was freshly manicured and decorated with light makeup and pink lip gloss. Lilly appeared much younger than her actual age with pleasant features, blue eyes and dark blonde shoulder length hair. She was slightly hefty with barrel legs and large thighs which made her look somewhat matronly.

Bill Smiley was a smooth talking intellectual in his

mid-sixties but still handsome with a full head of wavy

brown hair, brown eyes, light complexion, perfect Roman

nose, thin lips and square chin. He nurtured a congenial

personality and courteous manners. He welcomed Lilly to

his show and posed his first question:

"People generally refer to you as moderate liberal. Is that

how you would describe your political views?"

"Actually," Lilly answered with a cultured smile, "I

don't think of myself as either liberal or conservative. I

examine each individual issue affecting our American way

of life and consider all the pros and cons before taking a

stand one way or the other. I support those principles and

values that I believe are in the best interest of all our

citizens."

"How about abortion? When a mentally competent

woman or teenager becomes pregnant following voluntary

sexual intercourse, do you approve of killing the zygote or

the fetus in its mother's womb?"

Lilly first put forth the legal definition in Roe versus

Wade: "The United States Supreme Court has ruled that

life does not begin until the fetus is viable outside the

womb."

Bill would not let her evade his question. "I do not

care what some abortionists in Washington think. I want to

know whether you, Lilly, personally believe it is okay to

kill a zygote or fetus when the mother's life is not being

threatened by the baby growing inside her womb."

"As president, I would be sworn to uphold the law. The

law permits abortion up until the fetus is viable outside the

womb."

"Lilly, I am not asking what the law permits. I am asking

what you personally believe about killing a a zygote or

fetus that through the process of cellular mitosis and

genetic coding is quickly growing as a human being inside

it's own mother's womb."

Lilly carefully considered the question and what the next one might be. "I personally don't have a problem with abortion of unwanted and unloved infants prior to actual birthing."

"Unwanted and unloved by who, Lilly? There are countless childless couples who are begging to care for infants unwanted and unloved by natural mothers. I am not at this point including zygotes or fetuses pursuant to rape, incest, or posing danger to the mother or those fetuses physically or mentally handicapped. I am asking about a healthy zygote or fetus growing normally within its mother's womb. Why kill it. The mother doesn't have to care for it after birth, just give the baby to someone who will love and care for it. So, unwanted and unloved doesn't justify abortion. Do you have another reason for feeling comfortable with killing children in the womb?"

Lilly retreated to the viable outside the womb criteria

for human life. "I do not consider aborting a zygote or fetus

as killing children in the womb. I believe life begins when

the birthing process is complete and the fetus is viable

outside the womb; which just happens to be the law."

Bill pressed forward. "Life and law are two different

concepts. The law is a collection of rules and regulations

handed down by a king, dictator or elected law making

body like our Congress. Federal judges do not make law.

Under our federal constitution only Congress can enact a

law. State legislatures enacted anti-abortion laws. Federal

judges usurped the legislative function of sovereign states

and imposed their own biases and prejudices upon the

states which is absolutely forbidden by the tenth

amendment to our federal constitution. Life is defined by

scientists as the ability to move, feed and reproduce. Any

organic entity that exhibits these three characteristics has life by definition. The zygote and fetus move through cellular mitosis, feed off the mother's blood, and reproduce through genetic coding. The legal argument as to when life begins is mental masturbation to justify legal murder. A baby outside the womb is not viable without a substitution for the mother's blood nutrients. Milk or infant formula is required for the infant to be viable. So the viability issue is pure nonsense. In terms of killing the fetus, does it really matter whether you kill it during the first or third trimester or after birthing is completed?"

Lilly was anxious for the interview to conclude. "I am not in favor of partial birth abortion."

"Why not? If the fetus is not viable inside the womb and thus subject to being killed, then partial birth abortion is no different than killing the developing baby during the first or second trimester. Or, killing the live infant since it is not viable on its own."

"You're right, Bill. It really is a matter of semantics. But, at the present time abortion is legally protected and I am in favor of upholding the law."

Bill looked at her with sadness. "To me, it does not matter whether the fetus is burned alive with saline fluid or butchered halfway out of the birth canal. The embryo embedded in the womb is alive and every honest person knows that to be a fact. It is growing and being nourished by the mother's blood. Saying it is just a blob of tissue does not make it so."

Lilly looked stunned. "You're saying abortion is murder?"

Bill nodded in the affirmative. "That is exactly what I am saying. Consider the abortionist mindset. It is cold blooded and premeditated. The killer induces labor, then reaches inside the birth canal and jerks the fetus head first out of the vaginal opening exposing the baby's head and shoulders in order to murder the infant. Then a surgical

instrument is used to punch a hole in the baby's neck so

that its brain can be suctioned out. The quivering corpse of

the child is then pitched onto a disposal table from where it

is permanently disposed of. That, Lilly, is murder

regardless of how you try to excuse it by saying no...no....it

was just mommy exercising her right to free choice."

Lilly needed a moment to recover from Bill's

forthrightness. "You're describing partial birth abortion."

"Abortion is abortion, Lilly. It doesn't matter whether it

is partial birth abortion or first, second, or third trimester

abortion. The law you hide behind says it is okay to kill the

baby any time before the birth process is completed and the

baby is viable outside the womb. Political appointees in

their senile years wrapped in judicial robes bypassed our

law making process and imposed their partisan political

ideology upon us without any constitutional authority.

What I and more than a hundred million Americans want to know is whether you intend to support law making from the bench along political party lines rather than to insist upon the separation of powers specifically spelled out so that a fifth grade student can understand it within the plain wording of the Tenth Amendment to the United States Constitution?"

Lilly passed the buck. "The Congress has not seen fit to overturn Roe v. Wade by legislative action. When such a law is passed, I, as president, would stand behind Congress since Congress can limit the Supreme Court's jurisdiction."

Bill laughed softly. "That's not very likely since radical liberals control Congress now, and the majority of the Democratic politicians are abortionists. But, maybe the voters will wake up and change that majority to a minority."

Bill smiled politely. "Let's move on to the homosexual

agenda of the liberal Democrats. Do you think, Lilly, that

Sodom and Gomorrah was more morally depraved than the

United States is today?"

"Worse by what yardstick?"

"In terms of open homosexuality, violence, blasphemy

against God, child molestation, shamelessness, and same

sex marriage?" Bill cocked his left eyebrow in a

questioning manner and continued: "Although pertaining to

Sodom and Gomorrah there is no Scriptural indication that

homosexuals in those two cities practiced same sex

marriage. That is too far out even for Sodomites. What do

you think, Lilly?"

"I think what consenting adults do in the privacy of

their bedrooms and how they wish to legally bind

themselves is their business not mine."

Bill held up his hand like a stop sign. "We are not

talking about consenting adults behaving in private and

engaging in same sex copulation. We are talking about

reading homosexual romance stories to kindergarten

children; school teachers and youth leaders teaching

teenagers to sodomize each other; homosexuals rubbing

our noses in their sexual perversions and public ceremonies

mocking Christian morals and values. We are talking about

the most disgusting, repulsive, and reprehensible behavior

that human beings can imagine being shoved down our

throats by Congress, by the US Supreme Court, by the

liberal news media, and flaunted on prime time Television.

Are you, Lilly, in favor of brainwashing grammar school

children into accepting homosexual lifestyles and same sex

marriage?"

"Scientific studies find that same sex orientation is as

natural as heterosexual orientation. Homosexuals are born

with same sex orientation." Bill snickered with disgust.

"What scientific studies, Lilly. I have never seen any

scientific data proving same sex orientation to be genetically determined nor some sort of mutational defect. Same sex orientation is one of the ways abused and neglected children try to cope with neurotic personality development. Otherwise, homosexuals could not forsake such perversion and become healthy heterosexuals if same sex orientation is genetically driven or results from mutational happenstance.

Lilly considered the possibilities. "I am not a scientist. Neither am I a homosexual. I will leave sexual orientation to personal choice."

Bill saw a dead end ahead and decided to give Lilly a chance to defend teaching children that humans evolved from lower life forms. "In our public schools, Lilly, are you in favor of teaching children as scientific fact an outdated and totally impossible theory commonly referred to as Evolution?"

Lilly suspected that Bill could back up his statement that

the theory of evolution is physically impossible. She

sidestepped the question by pointing the finger at the

Supreme Court. "The United States Supreme Court has

ruled that special creation cannot be taught in our public

schools in order to maintain separation of church and

state."

Bill again flashed a polite smile. "Lilly, which of our

founding father's words are quoted to support the premise

that God and special creation cannot be taught in our public

schools?"

Lilly breathed somewhat easier. "Thomas Jefferson?"

Bill nodded in agreement. "Lilly, Thomas Jefferson ordered

the Bible used as a text book in our public schools. Church

services were routinely held in the Senate chamber.

Sessions of Congress began with a prayer. Our founding

documents are full of supplications to God. It was not until homosexuals, abortionists, and evolutionists began

infiltrating our schools, courts, and mass media that the

ACLU squandered millions of taxpayer dollars getting

laws passed by radical liberals to outlaw God in our public

forums. Are you, Lilly, in favor of delusional, ridiculous

and impossible teachings that mankind evolved from lower

life forms over eons of time."

Lilly again tried to pass the buck. "We have a lot of

very bright people including many scientists who accept

evolution as a scientific fact."

"What we have, Lilly, is a small minority of little

Lucifer's trying to usurp God's dominion just like their

lying father. I will give you four irrefutable reasons why

evolution of single-celled organisms into humans is

absolutely impossible: (1) irreducible levels of complexity

at the molecular level; (2) DNA coding is neither random

nor accidental; (3) if the current world population doubling time cycle is increased 300%, it would take just 6,000

years to reach the current global population; and (4) there

are not trillions of immediate life forms in the fossil record.

A proven intermediate life form has never been found

whereas billions of living creatures do appear in the same

geologic time window."

Lilly's panty hose were now sticking to her thighs. "I

am in favor of upholding the law, Bill. Currently, it is

illegal not to teach evolution in our public schools."

"That's my whole point, Lilly. Are you, if elected

president of the United States, going to support radical

Democratic agendas; or will you try to change ridiculous

judge-enacted laws that cater to a loud mouthed obnoxious

minority of abortionists, homosexuals and evolutionists

rather than seventy-five percent of the population of these

United States? Last time I checked, we are still a

democracy where the majority rules."

"It will take a majority to elect me president."

Bill nodded courteously. "Perhaps Forenborn can make that happen. Thank you, Lilly, for coming on the show, and I hope you decide to come back."

CHAPTER FOUR

Georgie Sorrow's mansion was buzzing with activity. Uniformed servants parked Cadillacs, Jaguars, Mercedes, Rolls Royces, Porches and other luxury automobiles; and opened doors for arriving limos as super rich and famous radicals flocked to Georgie's fund raising dinner for Barry Osama.

Inside the mansion, white coated waiters and waitresses flitted among the arriving guests and offered a variety of drinks and palate pleasing Hors d'oeuvres. Three distinct groups began to form and glad hand each other. Hollywood personalities greeted each other with warmth and affection. The politicians practiced their bafflegab while mentally undressing the women who were trying to show as much breasts and thighs as high society permits. Executives of previously conservative foundations converted by silver

spoon heirs to radical liberal agendas converged on

Georgie to pledge their unwavering support of his choice

for the Oval Office. Twenty dining tables with seating for

twelve guests each were furnished with delicate crystal,

gold and china place settings, fresh flowers and linen

napkins. The tables were arranged in a quadrangle in the

center of Georgie's gigantic dining room.

A total of thirty-six waiters and waitresses continued

serving drinks and Hors d'oeuvres while patiently waiting

for the guests to be seated. Group conversations were

subdued but lively and well mannered. Huddled in a tight

circle among the politicians were George Whitman, Meg

McGovern, Steve Campbell, Jerry Browning, and Tom

Poizner. Executives identified by their name tags were

present representing the Hides, Stonefeller, Phew,

Carnneggie, Hewlete, Bulit, McArther, Heenz, and Turnars

charitable foundations. Among the most liberal Hollywood

personalities were Ben Witman, Jim Robbing, Tim

Springsteed, Bruce Ketcher, Aston Foxy, Michael Reeves,

Christopher Frankin, and Brad Afleck.

Georgie Sorrow walked to the podium fifteen feet left of

the table quadrangle and adjusted the microphone to his

height. "Good evening, Ladies and Gentlemen. It is with

great appreciation that I welcome you all to my special

fund raising dinner for the next president of the United

States, Barry Osama." Every guest clapped with

enthusiastic smiles and head nodding.

"Please be seated so we can serve you. We have a

variety of beef, lamb and pork sauteed to perfection with

exquisite herbs and spices. Our entrees include filet

mignon, Peking Duck, quail, pheasant, and lamb to

complement your fresh salads, baked potatoes, and a

choice of ten other side dishes plus assorted breads. You

also have a choice of twenty dinner wines and French

Champagnes. An array of fine desserts have been prepared

by our gourmet chefs and will be served with ice cream

and your choice of the finest Columbian coffees ground

and sifted in our kitchen. I will return after dinner to

introduce our guest speakers for this evening."

Glen Ripuone looked into the cameras at Telitright News

and welcomed his viewers. He sported gray dress slacks,

beige sweater over a blue dress shirt, and black zippered

boots. Short blonde hair and sky blue eyes set off his

cherubim face. "Hello out there, all you twisted

conservative freaks. Sorrow and his disciples are having

dinner tonight plotting your demise and the death of

capitalism. Georgie and the morons around him with empty

heads and full pockets are greasing the skids they believe

will slide an African Muslim communist into the White

House. Georgie and the liberal elite stuffing their faces at

his mansion consider us conservatives to be an illiterate,

red necked, bigoted, racist minority. It is true that my math

is sometimes suspect, but I can definitely add percentages

that total one hundred. As I speak, independents and

conservatives still outnumber liberal radicals by a

sufficient margin to defeat Osama's bid for the presidency

of our democratic, capitalistic, free market, God loving

nation. But, we must act now."

Glen sighed and confessed a fact that few Americans

know. "We cannot indefinitely halt the conversion of

America into a socialistic and bankrupt beggar nation, but

we can push the fall of the United States beyond our

generation. In fact, we have already beaten the odds. About

the time that the Thirteen Colonies adopted our federal

constitution in 1787, Alexander Tyler, a Scottish history

professor at the University of Edinburgh, had this to say

about the fall of the Athenian Republic some 2,000 years

earlier:

"('A democracy is always temporary in nature; it simply

cannot exist as a permanent form of government. A

democracy will continue until the time that voters discover

they can vote themselves generous gifts from the public

treasury. From that moment on, the majority always votes

for the candidates who promise the most benefits from the

public treasury, with the result that every democracy will

finally collapse due to loose fiscal policy, which is always

followed by a dictatorship. The average age of the world's

greatest democracies from the beginning of history has

been about 200 years. During those two hundred years, the

democracies progressed through the following sequence:

from bondage to spiritual faith; from spiritual faith to great

courage; from courage to liberty; from liberty to

abundance; from abundance to complacency; from

complacency to apathy; from apathy to dependence; and

from dependency back into bondage.')"

Glen paused for effect, looked humbly into the main

camera and continued: "Professor Joseph Olson, Hamline

University Law School, points out the difference between

urban welfare and overburdened taxpayers:

('Politicians, mostly from the radically liberal

Democratic Party, have pilfered our national treasury to

buy votes from those among us who prefer dependence to

liberty not knowing that dependency quickly leads to

bondage and oppression. The conservative Republican

Party generally carries 29 states and the Democrats only

19. Square miles of land with a Democratic majority is

roughly half a million compared to 2.4 million square

miles for Republicans. Total population of counties won by

Republicans is approximately 143 million to 127 million

for counties supporting Democrats. The murder rate for

Republican counties is 2.1 per 100,000 and 13.2 for

Democratic counties. In aggregate, the map of territory

won by Republicans is mostly the land owned by the

taxpaying citizens of this great country. Democrat territory

mostly encompasses those citizens living in government

owned tenements and living off various forms of

government welfare.....').

Glen nodded sadly. "Today, we know that some forty

odd percent of the nation's population has already reached

the government dependency phase. What comes next is

going back into bondage. That is exactly where Georgie

Sorrow and the man from Mombosa are planning on

leading America through bankrupting our nation. Why, you

may ask, would anyone in their right mind want to return

to bondage ruled by a dictator? It is the 'god complex' that

turned Satan into the adversary of God. Satan's children,

like the Sorrows and the Osamas of this nation, have the

same god complex as their spiritual father. They are power

mad egomaniacs who care for nothing but ruling over

everyone else. They are the political trash and human scum

of this planet exploiting the greedy welfare parasites who

now number above forty percent of total United States

citizens That percentage will expand under an Osama

presidency because Georgie and Barry's strategic plan is to

place enormous economic demands on a shrinking number

of taxpayers. Thereby, they plan to collapse capitalism and

the free market by fiscal policies that put more and more

citizens on the public dole while at the same time

maintaining porous borders allowing illegal aliens to flood

into America to ensure a voting majority fed and housed by

the taxpaying minority."

The main camera focused momentarily upon the U.S.

national debt monitor which exceeded seventeen trillion

dollars as Glen continued: "These shiftless and uneducated

aliens will mostly become minimum wage employees who

most certainly will vote to keep those in power who are

raiding the public treasury to care for them as U.S.

government wards. These millions of illegal immigrants

will place an onerous burden upon our currently

overburdened entitlement programs and accelerate

America's descent into oblivion. We currently owe

including our continuously expanding and unfunded

entitlement programs more than 116 trillion dollars which

is nearly twice as much as the combined gross national

product of every nation in the world. Sorrow, Obama, and

the radical liberals who have infiltrated our Congress,

courts, schools and media intend to intentionally push

America into an economic free fall wherein our dollar

becomes more and more devalued. When it is to their

advantage, Asian nations will stop buying our debt and our

economy will disintegrate. The demise of the United States

will throw the entire world into economic chaos ushering

in a global government and a communist dictatorship to

allocate and distribute the necessities of life. Yes, indeed!!

You twisted conservative freaks, that is precisely what is

being planned at the Sorrow mansion this very night."

Back at the mansion, the guests were finishing up

dessert and after dinner drinks. A din of conversations

colored with laughter and hand gestures filled the dining

room. The covey of waiters and waitresses were busily

servicing the tables. Georgie Sorrow walked again to the

podium and addressed his well fed guests:

"Again, I thank one and all for accepting my invitation

and trust you will bear with me as I understand that our

guest of honor is running a little behind schedule. We'll

give Barry a chance to speak when he arrives. In the

meanwhile, I will turn the podium over to our first speaker,

Mr. Jim Robbing, famous Hollywood actor and my good friend."

Georgie stepped back clapping and the guests rose to their feet, clapping dutifully and then sitting down again. Robbing walked briskly to the podium waving enthusiastically at those present. "Thank you Georgie. Wow! Was that good food or what?"

The guests again clapped in unison. Georgie beamed and took a seat a few feet left of the podium. Robbing has gotten somewhat pudgy with puffy cheeks, slightly red nose and unruly brown hair. His tux looked a bit tight. "What can I say? You all know I'm a flaming liberal and great admirer of our gracious host. I won't bore you with personal trivia but I do want to comment on how we are going to transform America into a land of opportunity for those who are now being oppressed and exploited. It is neither fair nor logical that one who has made no contribution to society should live in vulgar luxury while

those who toil endlessly live in slumlord tenements. Every

citizen has a right to quality food, decent housing, graduate

school, reliable transportation and quality health care. In

order for us to make this happen we must narrow the gap

between the very rich and the poverty level working class.

We must lower the taxes on the working class and increase

the tax on those with incomes exceeding $200,000 a year.

Currently, eighty percent of America's wealth is controlled

by less than fifteen percent of the population. This ratio

must be adjusted by redistribution of the tax burden; by

national health care; by more student financial aid; and

accelerated opportunities for poverty level citizens."

Robbing held up a personal check to indicate his

contribution.

"I am more than willing to shoulder additional taxes on

my personal income in order to provide a better standard of

living for American workers. They are indispensable to the

prosperity of our great nation. Tonight, I am pledging the

maximum allowable contribution to help elect Barry

Osama to the presidency of the United States of America.

Thank you very much."

The dinner crowd rose in unison to give Robbing a

standing ovation. Georgie returned to the podium with an

angelic smile while Robbing retreated to his seat. "I will

join Jim Robbing in pledging the maximum contribution.

Who among you will stand with us?"

Every guest stood up signaling their personal pledge.

Georgie looked around with controlled ecstasy. He had just

raised over a million dollars in one evening for Barry

Osama. There were four more speakers to be heard but the

political dinner already exceeded his expectations. No one

was going to publicly pledge more than the maximum

allowable campaign contribution. His job was finished for

tonight. He would twist some arms later to raise another

ten million or so.

Jim McPaign and Sarah Planke sipped coffee together

aboard a chartered jetliner bound for Pittsburgh. Jim had

just turned seventy-two and Sarah had recently celebrated

her forty-fifth birthday. Although squat and partially bald,

Jim was still in good physical condition except for crippled

arms due to being tortured as a POW in Vietnam. Sarah

radiated refined beauty with long dark hair, clean sparkling

face, amber eyes and very nice curves, especially for the

mother of five children. She noticed the far away look in

Jim's eyes. "Ever think when you were being brutalized in

Vietnam that you might run for president of the nation you

fought for?"

"Not really. I thought mostly about staying alive and

how to cope with repetitive abuse and physical pain."

Jim's voice sounded detached and void of emotion. "I was amazed at the level of torture I could endure while concentrating on my family back home and on my fellow prisoners also being abused. Man's inhumanity to man can be very frightening."

Sarah reached out and squeezed his hand. "You were faithful to America. I am very proud to be chosen as your running mate. I learned a bit of political savvy as governor of my state, but I'll need a lot of guidance from you on running for vice president."   Jim smiled sympathetically. "You know as much about running for vice president as I do about running for president. But, one thing I'm pretty sure about. People are most likely to vote for you because they like you rather than your campaign rhetoric. So, that's what I recommend. Let's get the voters to like us better than the opposition. Let's just be ourselves and avoid phony impressions. I picked you because you are very bright, very pretty, and very family oriented. You have

more executive experience than Barry Osama without

being arrogant or flippant. Barry is a gifted orator but

brings a lot of dirty laundry with him to the campaign trail.

Let's let the conservative media highlight his negatives

while we concentrate on our positives. I've been in

Congress over twenty years and you have governed our

largest state. I think we complement each other quite well."

Sarah's apprehensions dwindled. "I agree, Jim. I don't

like dirty politics, and I sincerely appreciate your

confidence in me. I won't let you down."

Jojo Hiden and Barry Osama shared two common flaws.

Neither had ever accomplished anything worth reflecting

upon. They were also flip flopping oily politicians with no

pleasing personality traits whatsoever other than skillful

parroting of a professional speech writer's thoughts

displayed on a teleprompter.

Barry was much better than Jojo in voice control and measured tones. He may have learned public speaking demagoguery at his Forenborn podium. Now, at age 47, he had not managed or directed anything. He claimed to have spent some limited time teaching constitutional law (mainly how best to circumvent the constitution) and also as a minority token hire at a prestigious law firm. His most outstanding accomplishment had been teaching Saul Alinsky's Rules For Radicals to recruits for Forenborn, an organization of alleged community organizers.

Forenborn was dedicated to stirring up racial tension and ripping off the taxpayers to fund real estate loans for people unable to make the payments, and more government entitlement programs for those who could draw more in welfare than full time employment based on accumulated education and training.

Nonetheless, Barry had been vaunted into the Senate by

the rich and liberal manipulators within the Chicago

political machine where he worked behind the scenes with

the likes of Georgie Sorrow to lay the financial foundation

for a run at the White House.

Consequently, an African native with zero experience

managing or directing any type of business, organization or

enterprise; no experience whatsoever in free market

economics, foreign policy, military training or statesman-

ship became the favorite son and presidential candidate for

the Democratic party. The folks referred to by Barry

Osama as being exploited, underprivileged and oppressed;

being mostly wards of the government with plenty of idle

time to eat, drink, smoke dope and copulate; were fast

becoming the majority of voters in America. Yeah! Barry

would keep the freebies coming and tax the fat cats

providing employment for American workers.

Jojo had been in the United States Senate for over

twenty years. He was likeable enough: slim physique, gray

headed, steely eyed, well dressed, benevolent features, and

better than average orator. Having never accomplished

anything but fill a Senate seat and bad mouth the other

party, Jojo was the perfect running mate for Barry Osama.

Jojo traveled freely on the taxpayer's dime and convinced

many liberals like himself that being a world traveler had

somehow conveyed upon him a great understanding of the

most complex foreign policy issues. Georgie Sorrow and

Willie Bombsetter were pretty confident that Jojo could

steer Barry away from poor foreign policy decisions.

Barry and Jojo relaxed with after dinner drinks and

discussed campaign strategy aboard a modified Boeing 707

en route to Detroit, Michigan. Jojo stroked his chin and

looked quizzically at Barry. "We gotta talk more about

major change in Washington. That's McPaign's main

campaign issue. No more business as usual; legislation to

control lobbyists; eliminate pork barrel projects; lower

taxes; and balance the budget. We gotta steal his thunder

while reminding voters at every stop that the Republicans

had eight years to accomplish what they're preaching now.

All McPaign is gonna do is give America four more years

of the failed Hush administration policies." Jojo drained

his glass like he had just delivered the Gettysburg Address.

He smacked his lips and waited for Barry's recognition of

his keen insight.

Barry looked at Jojo thoughtfully. "I suspect that

McPaign will be astute enough to remind the voters that the

Democrats controlled Congress during eight of the last

twelve years and did nothing to head off the financial crisis

triggered by us radicals coercing banks into extending

millions of housing loans to people who couldn't pay their

rent. Yes, we'll keep hammering Hush about allowing an

economic meltdown and favoring fat cat bankers and the

big oil companies. We'll also keep beating the drum about

the wars dragging on and on in Afghanistan and Iraq and

how much that is costing the taxpayers. We'll ridicule and

mock him and keep the Republicans on the defensive. High

unemployment and public panic favor us. We can use the

economic crisis to our advantage while buying time to push

more voters into dependence on government handouts. The

public will accept our projection that economic recovery

will be slow and painful because of the monumental

problems inherited from Hush."

Barry drained his glass and handed it to Jojo for a refill.

"We'll champion amnesty, welfare and citizenship for

illegal aliens and encourage more immigration across the

Rio Grande. We'll openly promise redistribution of wealth

by cutting taxes on the poor and raising taxes on the rich

capitalists. We'll promise the poor and underprivileged

government funded health care and more government

financial assistance. We'll promise heaven on Earth and

blame every time delay on sweeping up after Hush. We'll

keep repeating that Hush took eight years to drive the

economy into the ground and we can't be expected to fix

the problems overnight."

Not being the brightest politician in the Senate, Jojo

couldn't quite figure out how Barry was going to save the

economy by destroying the free market and taxing the rich

who were already paying approximately eighty percent of

all taxes collected by the IRS. Didn't Barry understand that

the rich capitalists would simply invest their money in

other countries if taxed beyond reason? Then, who was

going to pay for all the government freebies.? They would

be promising the voters something they could not possibly

deliver. America already owed more than the combined

wealth of the entire world. Didn't they teach basic

economics at Harvard?

Slowly, it dawned upon Jojo that he had hooked up with a very dangerous socialist radical bent on converting capitalism into communism in exchange for personal gratification. He needed another drink.

"When the rich remove their wealth from the economy, what happens then?" Barry laughed inwardly at Jojo's thick skull. "Then, Mr. Vice President, the public will be forced to accept global government where the poor get a bigger share and the rich pay the tab. The collapse of American democracy will trigger world-wide pandemonium because American gluttony supports the economies of other nations. The United States now consumes a fourth of the wealth of the entire world and we are the biggest customer of our biggest creditors. The world cannot soon recover from the disintegration of America. The proof of that premise has been demonstrated by the bursting of the housing credit bubble. When major US financial institutions began going belly up, the entire world was

thrown into an economic panic. Left alone, over time, the

free market will recover. It is in the interim time frame that

global government will be welcomed by billions of hungry

people in all nations. In the meanwhile, we can pilfer

billions that can't be traced when global confusion runs

rampant. But, the paper must be traded for precious metals

while the paper has value. When we get control of both

Congress and the White House, we become the keepers of

the treasury."

Jojo glanced around nervously and breathed easier

when he noted there was no one else close enough to

overhear their conversation. His stomach flip flopped.

Barry was actually plotting the fall of America. But, why

tell him? Then, he began to see the bigger picture. Barry's

scenario was no secret among the radical liberals. Such had

been their unspoken game plan since FDR. Each Democratic administration brought the United States farther

along the path to self destruction. Nikata Kruschev's

famous prediction was coming to pass. American was

destroying itself from within. Those content to vote

themselves gifts from the pubic treasury were becoming

the majority of voters. American democracy was now

doomed along with the free market. Well, he might as well

take advantage of the opportunity presented while he had

the chance. But, a possibility flashed through his alcohol

deadened mind.

"What if we get booted and a new administration simply

refuses to honor our debts. Kinda like when Russia refused

to pay their war debt to the United States?"

Barry couldn't stifle an ironic laugh. "That's the whole

point, Jojo. The United States couldn't pay our debt over

the short term under any circumstances. All of our

entitlement programs are a gigantic Ponzi scheme. The

wealth to pay the debt doesn't exist. We can't fund welfare,

Medicare, Social Security and nationalized health care plus

other government subsidies to feed and house the

unemployed and the unemployable more than a couple of

fiscal years. Do you realize that just the interest on our

current debt is approaching half the entire gross national

product of Russia? Our national debt including the

entitlement programs feeding and housing half the

population of the nation is roughly double the wealth of the

entire world. Moreover, when the Ponzi bubbles burst,

there won't be any capitalists left to provide jobs which

means no public treasury. That's why we have to raid it

now and squirrel away non-paper wealth to be at the top of

the elite oligarchy."

Jim McPaign and Sarah Planke waved to a huge crowd

from a hastily constructed wooden platform in Pittsburgh.

There were ten microphones strung along the platform walkway and each candidate held one chin high. A chilly wind whipped across the walkway prompting Jim and Sarah to raise their coat collars.

"Thank you! Thank you," Jim shouted. "Are we ready to take on corruption in Washington?" The crowd numbering over 30,000 screamed with approval, stomped their feet, whistled and clapped wildly. Thousands waved miniature American flags and posters supporting the Republican ticket. Sarah and Jim beamed with appreciation and waved back until the noise level dropped. Then, Jim continued: "Are we ready to cut taxes, balance the budget and create more jobs?" Again the crowd roared approval. Sarah yelled into her microphone: "Are we ready to produce cheap energy from our own wells and stop supporting Muslim dictators? At this question, the crowd went wild with enthusiasm.

"We've got it!!" Sarah yelled back. "Let's drill for it!!"

The noisy approval from the crowd drowned out all other sounds. Jim and Sarah smiled and waved until they could be heard again. Then, Sarah held her microphone very close to her lips and spoke slowly for emphasis: "Now, folks, I want you to hold your applause and listen very, very carefully to what I want every individual here to know."

Sarah waited until the people became silent. Her face became flush with passion. "There is no oil shortage!!!" She bellowed out. "But, there is a devastating shortage of honest investors, developers, speculators and politicians. We are being raped without mercy by special interest groups joining hands with foreign mercenaries to steal us blind." Sarah continued without notes or teleprompter:

"Those trying to destroy America have conjured up a crisis which I will try to summarize for you. The most reliable source today for estimating the known oil reserves

around the world is the U.S. Geological Survey and actual

production has demonstrated the published reserves to be

grossly underestimated. We have as of today explored for

oil less than one third of earth's underground repositories

and we continue to find previously unknown reserves.

However, let's limit our thinking to known oil reserves

which fall into two categories: reserves recoverable with

existing technology and reserves recoverable with

advanced technology. Total reserves are underestimated at

approximately eight trillion barrels, of which roughly two

trillion can be recovered with existing technology.

Currently, the world consumption is about thirty billion

barrels per year. Simple division of two trillion by thirty

billion means that at the current consumption rate we have

enough oil consistent with current affordable technology to

last sixty-six years. With financially feasible advanced

technology, we have enough oil reserves for another one

hundred and thirty two years; and we have yet to explore

two thirds of the possible oil reserves in the earth. Yes!! We

are being lied to, manipulated, brainwashed and led like

sheep to the slaughter."

An amazed hush enveloped the entire gathering. People

stared at each other in total astonishment. A defiant

rumbling rippled through the assembly and became a

deafening cry of anger. Sarah waited with a solemn

expression until the people quieted down to hear more.

"Yes, I do clearly understand that emerging industrial

powers like China will increase world oil consumption,

But, even if consumption doubles, we have enough

reserves to fuel world economies for another ninety-nine

years if there are no more undiscovered reserves in

existence which is highly unlikely. Don't you think ninety-

nine years is an adequate time window to make financially

feasible the transformation of plentiful combustible gases like oxygen, hydrogen, methane, propane, and a byproduct of oil production, natural gas, into energy sources to replace petroleum products? We are right now burning off natural gas at the well heads which will today power motor vehicles with modest engineering changes. Oil prices are being artificially propped up to enrich those conning us."
Sarah nodded up and down.

"Yeah. Yeah. I know. Another group of lying, greedy pigs are getting filthy rich giving you a snow job about global warming. Yes. Indeed! The nasty, obnoxious, toxic, carbon dioxide is super heating the atmosphere. The polar ice caps are going to melt and raise the oceans two feet. The polar bears are going to die off and intermittent droughts are going to starve us all to death. Hey, people! Are we imbeciles? It is snowing in the desert. Polar bears are multiplying freely. We are enduring unseasonably frigid temperatures. The planet has been cooling for a decade. We

are paying farmers not to grow food crops. Carbon dioxide

provides oxygen for us to breathe. Plants, trees, grass, and

myriad varieties of vegetation absorb carbon dioxide and

give off oxygen. Politicians are generally not climatol-

ogists. The scare mongers fleecing us are eliminating water

vapor from graphs and statistics depicting global warming.

If we humans halted all production of food, energy,

manufacturing and transportation, there would be no

meaningful change in global temperatures because water

vapor which we cannot control actually determines global

temperature variations."

The crowd was so stunned that the noise level remained

constant. Sarah continued. "Having said all that, I am very

much in favor of replacing oil as our primary energy

source. It is a pollutant that affects our air quality and

transporting it poses a threat to pristine waters, our

beaches, and our wild life. But, there is no oil shortage.

That is a manufactured myth for the single purpose of

picking our pockets. Jim has a suggestion about how to

stop the thievery."

Sarah stepped back and smiled at Jim. The crowd went

absolutely bananas. Jim and Sarah smiled and waved and

smiled and waved. Finally, Jim could be heard. "Is this

lady tough or what!!! My suggestion can be very simply

stated. Go to the polls and send some public servants to

Washington that you can trust."

Jim and Sarah smiled and waved. The enthusiastic

reaction of the assembly could be heard for miles in all

directions. After the crowd vented for a couple of long

minutes, Jim raised his microphone to his lips and signaled

with his left hand that he wanted to continue:

"Liberals want to grant amnesty to illegal aliens violating

our laws and our borders. The more illegal immigrants, the

more eventual liberal Democratic votes. Let's compare the liberal political strategy to the response of other nations regarding the problem of illegal aliens." Jim grinned ear to ear.

"If you cross the North Korean border illegally, you get twelve years hard labor.

If you cross the Iranian border illegally, you are detained indefinitely.

If you cross the Afgan border illegally, you get shot.

If you cross the Saudi Arabian border illegally, you get thrown in jail.

If you cross the Chinese border illegally, you may never be heard from again.

If you cross the Venezuela border illegally, you will be branded a spy and your fate will be sealed.

If you cross the Cuban border illegally, you will be thrown into political prison to rot.

If you cross the United States border illegally, you get:
a job; a driver's license, a social security card; welfare;
food stamps; credit cards; subsidized rent or a loan to buy a
house; a free education; free health care; a lobbyist in
Washington; billions of dollars worth of public documents
printed in your language; the right to carry your country's
flag while you protest U.S. policies; community organizers
to help you get false identification and register to vote; and
the chance to work for a rich politician and pay no taxes."

Jim lowered his microphone temporarily and looked
slowly around the assembly. "So, why would any
uneducated, unemployed, hungry, illegal alien want to
sneak across our border and become a United States
government ward? Can anybody here figure it out?"

The crowd responded with a mixture of laughter and
rage. Someone screamed: "Throw the bums out!!" In
unison the crowd began chanting: "Throw the bums out!!

Throw the bums out!! Throw the bums out!!"

Jim and Sarah smiled and waved for a full three minutes

and then Sarah stepped forward and indicated she wanted

to speak. The crowd quieted down.

"I am extremely proud to be Senator's McPaign's choice

for Vice President. The liberal media says I don't have

enough experience to run for vice president. That's because

they want to make the news rather than report it, just like

liberal judges want to enact laws from the bench rather

than uphold laws enacted by Congress. They fawn and

swoon over Barry Osama who has zero executive

experience. He spent a couple of years as the freshman

senator from Illinois and spent most of that time campaign-

ing for higher office. The liberal media can't say enough

about Osama's fabulous experience as a community

organizer. That is because there is nothing else to talk

about. He has never managed, directed or governed any

sort of organization or business. What exactly is a

community organizer? Community organizers are radical

liberal activists funded by your tax dollars who stir up

racial tensions, demand more welfare and entitlement

programs, and coerce financial institutions into extending

credit to people who cannot repay the loans." Sarah shook

her fist in the air as she continued:

"Community organizers are primarily responsible for the

current financial crisis in America. Barry Osama taught

community organizer recruits how to coerce, ridicule, and

mock those who believe in the very concepts that have

made America the most envied nation on Earth. Commun-

ity organizers are dedicated to destroying the free market,

capitalism and individual incentives. Saul Alinsky's Rules

For Radicals is the bible for community organizers. That is

what Osama taught Forenborn recruits. By his own

admission, he has no management or executive experience

other than teaching Rules For Radicals. The liberal media

wants to convince you that serving as a Forenborn

instructor is a monumental achievement that uniquely

qualifies Osama for president of the United States." Sarah

paused, shrugged and laughed.

"Now, I freely admit that serving as both mayor and

governor constitutes my previous public service. As

governor of our largest energy producing state, I command-

ed the state's military forces and managed a nine billion

dollar budget. Thus, I have more executive experience that

most members of Congress and certainly much more than

Barry Osama. However, I am not on the Republican ticket

because of my vast political experience. I am supporting

Senator McPaign in his dedication to change the way

Washington does business: to put your interests above pork

barrel vote buying and big campaign contribution from

lobbyists for special interest groups; to return some sanity to government spending and runaway deficits; and to

strengthen both our economy and military capabilities. The

liberal media getting thrills up their legs from Osama's

bafflegab is concerned more with my wardrobe and my

hunting skills than Osama's lack of any executive

experience whatsoever. They attack my daughter's

pregnancy more than Osama's senatorial votes to murder

infants who survive abortion attempts and are born alive."

Sarah's tone became scalding.

"Osama wants to kill such babies instead of allowing

foster parents to love and care for them. The liberal media

is saturated with hard core socialists and communists. They

attack me as a wife and mother and mock me for not

aborting a handicapped son. They ignore the fact Osama

was conceived out of wedlock; that his paternal

grandmother says he was born in Keyna, Africa; that he

associates with known terrorists, criminals, and

communists; that his wife surrendered her license to

practice law; that he was mentored for twenty years by a

raving, racist, black militant preacher serving as his

substitute father; that he swore to be foreign born in order

to get financial aid; and that he wants to play Robin Hood

by robbing the productive, hard working, taxpaying

American citizens to fund government freebies for those

who won't work and who pay no taxes." The crowd roared

with rage and then let Sarah finish:

"Jim and I just recently discussed running on the issues

and not the undesirable backgrounds of our opponents.

Well, I'm serving notice right now to the liberal media and

the Osama campaign. Stop insulting my family and

mocking my moral values lest I really stand up and tell it

like it is. Now, folks, let's stick with the tough issues

affecting all American patriots and send a man to the White

House who will both represent and defend your interests."

The crowd exploded with support while Jim and Sarah

smiled and waved, and smiled and waved.

The white stone fireplace in Georgie Sorrow's private

office blazed with pine logs giving off a pleasing odor.

Georgie and Barry Osama were alone except for a few

servants who lived at the mansion. Secret Service agents

stood guard outside. Both men were casually dressed

befitting their financial status. They nursed their third drink

and discussed campaign strategy.

Georgie pulled on his throat skin with his right thumb

and forefinger and gazed at Barry. "That was a powerful

and convincing speech Sarah Planke delivered in

Pittsburgh this morning. She is much more talented and

effective than I ever imagined. We have to shut her down

pronto."

Barry vigorously shook his head in agreement. "I've put

out the word to all our media friends. They'll send

investigators to her home town and sniff out her back-

ground from birth. A strong willed woman like Sarah

surely made some enemies on the way to mayor and

governor. We'll paint her as a backwoods bitch and

McPaign as a rich snob who can't identify with mainstream

America. We can also hammer his wife about inheriting all

that money from beer distributorships and buying multiple

homes rather than making charitable donations for the poor

and underprivileged."

Georgia stared into the flames. "That's a start, but we

need more. McPaign is seventy-two and if elected he

would be the oldest man ever to serve as a first term

president. We can spook the public about the possibility of

him dying in office and Planke becoming president. She

has no foreign policy experience just like you. But, we put

a man on your ticket that the public will accept as a foreign policy expert. Jojo served several terms as chairman for

Congressional committees heavily involved in foreign

relations and military issues. One of McPaign's biggest

personal weaknesses is his lack of understanding as to how

the economy is affected by all the multiple factors driving

it. You can ambush him with specific questions about the

economy and make him appear inept. He is brutally honest

and will probably admit that he needs tutoring in free

market economics. Now, you don't have an economic

background either, so never answer a question about

something you don't fully understand. When asked such

questions, you already know precisely how to answer: poke

fun at the questioner; ridicule the nature of the question;

and never commit yourself. Put the opposition on the

defensive and then change the subject to some related issue

that you can bluff your way through. McPaign won't do

that. He'll either confess his lack of experience or try to

answer the question. Either way, he will expose his

weakness."

Georgie sipped his drink while Barry nodded agree-

ment. "I learned with some wonderment that if you laugh

off the question, people will go along with a change of

subject. Laughter and ridicule works every time. I often use

that technique on Jemama."

Georgie chuckled and then rubbed his chin thoughtfully.

"Getting back to overall campaign strategy, we must keep

the focus very narrow and loaded with emotional appeal.

We need a majority of votes and seventy-five percent of

voters in American are living on family incomes less than

$68,000 dollars. These are the people who decide who will

run the government. The emotional appeal must be specifi-

cally tailored to them. But, forty-two percent of the voters

do not earn enough to qualify for income taxes. We must

promise this 40% more government assistance and more

freebies; and guarantee the other 35% lower taxes while

increasing the tax contribution by families with incomes

exceeding $250,000. In between the $68,000 level and the

$250,000 level are the small businesses which employ the

majority of American workers." Georgie gave more advice

when Barry made no comment.

"Therefore, our primary campaign rhetoric must focus

on lower taxes for families earning less than $250,000;

higher taxes on families earning over $250,000; and more

government freebies for everyone else funded by higher

taxes on the fat cats like me. Then, to give us four aces to

McPaign's pair of deuces, we pander to the gay rights and

same sex marriage advocates; the pro-choice supporters;

and the anti-war movement. These are the passionate

dissidents who vote faithfully; so we can pull a majority of

them away from the Republicans because McPaign

vacillates on these emotion laden issues. We will insist that our tax policies will create more jobs, turn the economy

around, and provide more opportunity for the working

class. We'll bring the wars in Afghanistan and Iraq to an

end by better management and save billions to reduce the

budget deficit. We'll use smarter diplomacy and more

effective foreign policies to diminish terrorism and

discourage the spread of nuclear weapons." Georgie

finished off his drink and chuckled.

"The fact that we cannot deliver on these campaign

promises is immaterial. Once we get into office and make

more voters wards of the government, we can perpetuate a

voting majority." Osama also drained his glass, stood up

and shook Georgie's hand warmly. "You know how much I

value your advice. You're also making it possible for me to

spend McPaign into the ground. I owe you a great deal."

Georgie stood up and hugged Barry affectionately. "We're

both doing humanity a great service."

CHAPTER FIVE

Ivan Stylin, president of WOWU, and Howe Snicker, Osama's public relations consultant, were seated across from Bill Smiley as his Gottcha Show got under way. Ivan displayed his usual pasty scowl and Howie adjusted his designer glasses atop his hawkish nose. His straight black hair draped across his brow and his boyish cheeks framed a wide sullen mouth and rounded chin. He wore a gray suit and pink tie which contrasted with Ivan's jeans and pullover sweater.

Bill flashed his usual courteous smile and welcomed them to the show. He addressed his first question to Ivan. "It is rumored, Ivan, that Workers of the World Unite has raised over twenty-five million dollars for the Osama campaign. Is that a fairly accurate estimate?"

Ivan raised his eyebrows, wrinkled his nose and scratched at his right ear. "Yeah. I would say so. Give or take a couple hundred grand. But, that is peanuts from a membership of 2.1 million workers.....about twelve bucks per member. And, the members sent in personal contributions. The union itself contributed the maximum legal donation of $5,000."

Bill didn't blink. "What are WOWU members and Ivan Stylin expecting in return for this twenty-five million dollars in individual and union donations?" Ivan maintained his deadpan expression. "We just wanna see a man get elected president who in not anti-union. We think Barry Osama qualifies."

"Well, that's a reasonable and legal objective. For a fleeting moment I thought you might be lobbying for eliminating the secret ballot in an election among workers at a particular company as to whether they wanted to

unionize. Forgive me for my crassness."

Ivan shrugged slightly. "You're forgiven. We union guys

are quick to forgive people for being mistaken." Bill

couldn't stifle an amused chuckle. "Tell me, Ivan, what

would truly make you and WOWU happy?"   Ivan grinned

widely. "An equitable share of the value of goods and

services we produce."

"Ivan, you're getting more than an equitable share now.

WOWU members generally are employed within labor

intensive businesses. For each dollar in business revenue,

roughly forty-eight cents is paid to workers and to cover

employer taxes for social security, medicare and

unemployment insurance. About twelve cents goes to

management, engineering, and sales. Approximately nine

cents is spent for miscellaneous materials and operating

supplies. Nearly ten cents goes to cover required facilities and stockholder equity. Eleven cents goes to provide

medical insurance and other fringe benefits for workers.

The ten cents left out of the revenue dollar goes to net

before tax profit for the business. The business pays four

cents of that ten cents in income tax, state tax, and

municipal tax. So WOWU workers take eight times more

out of the business than the business owners who take all

the risks of loss. Do you want the business owners' nickel

too?"

Ivan looked both puzzled and defiant. "Where did you

get those numbers?" Bill lifted a stack of notes. "From the

IRS and the Department of Labor. The numbers are

averages for all business classified as labor intensive."

Ivan squinted at Bill. "How is a labor intensive business

defined?"

"A business that spends forty cents or more of each

revenue dollar on labor in the form of wages and

incentives. The average after tax profit for such business operations is five to six cents out of each revenue dollar. That is why investors are putting their money in foreign countries where labor is much cheaper. That is also why the United States is becoming uncompetitive in the world market."

Ivan squirmed noticeably. "I don't believe those bullshit numbers. Major corporations rake in billions in quarterly profits." Bill laughed softly. "Ivan, that is due to their world wide sales. They employ thousands of people and take in fifteen to twenty times more revenue dollars than after tax profit dollars. It is all relative to the scale of operations. Capital intensive businesses employ fewer workers than labor intensive businesses and therefore earn a larger return on investment. Workers in capital intensive businesses also take more of each revenue dollar than the investors and stockholders."

Ivan gave Bill a cocky look. "No business producing goods and services can operate without workers. We are as important as capital." Bill shrugged. "I did not insinuate otherwise. I am simply pointing out that if workers get more of the revenue dollar than they are now taking, there would be nothing left for the owners, investors and stockholders. There would be zero incentive for anyone to invest in a business which provides American jobs. The money will be invested in foreign countries."

Ivan showed his true colors. "Every citizen has a right to an equal share of the wealth of his or her native country." Bill laughed out loud. "I suspected you to be a serious communist, Ivan. Give me one example where communism has succeeded in distributing equal wealth to every citizen. Communism has never worked and never will. That is because communism destroys individual incentive and personal motivation. People will not take risks and sacrifice when they can earn no more than the

those who take no risks and exert minimum effort on the

job. " Bill looked at Ivan without blinking and added:

"The Soviet Union enforced communism with guns

until the Russian people finally revolted due to bread lines

and a collapsing economy. Red China now wants to

practice capitalism instead of communism because

communism produced a stagnant Chinese economy just

like it has always done where it has been tried." Ivan

became more defiant. "That is because the elite class has

lived like monarchs and forced the communist workers to

feed their gluttonous appetites. Communism managed by

the workers themselves has never been tried."

"Ivan, that is because workers who have learned

management skills want to run a capitalistic business. We

see that truth clearly in Russia and China." Bill turned

away from Ivan. "Let's give Howe a chance to talk about

advising Osama on public relations. What would you

recommend, Howe, concerning the issue of eliminating the

secret ballot during an election among a company's

workers pertaining to unionization?"

Howe Snicker was prone to answer very ambiguously

or to evade the question by resorting to mockery and

ridicule. Howe was pretty sure such strategy would nor

work with Bill Smiley. "Our next president favors

anything that brings about a better standard of living for

union workers as well as non-union workers." Bill

frowned wryly. "That's like saying communism is good for

the workers but capitalism is also good for the workers.

Which way do you cast your vote, Howe? Do you support

elimination of the secret ballot during union elections?"

Howe braced for a brutal thumping. He had been

apprehensive about appearing on Smiley's talk show and

now he knew it was a serious mistake. He had given in to

Osama's prompting to put Smiley in his place by a display

of his wit and intellectual superiority. "I think the question

of whether a secret ballot is utilized is really less than

significant. What is very important is that every worker

gets a chance to speak up and to vote."

Bill laughed with slight irritation at Howe's cheap dodge.

"Howe, secret ballots in union elections are just as essential

as secret ballots in presidential elections. The purpose of a

secret ballot is to lessen the threat of violence by thugs and

mental midgets during local and national elections against

those casting unpopular votes. Union thugocracy is

precisely why the National Labor Relations Board man-

dated secret ballots for unionization elections. Now,

Howe, are you, or are you not, advising Barry Osama to

champion elimination of the secret ballot in unionization

elections in order to increase the probability of a union

victory?"

Howe answered smugly: "Aren't you simply assuming

that elimination of secret ballots will favor unionization.

Do you have any facts to support your assumption? When

advising our next president, I have to rely on facts not

assumptions or personal opinions." Almost immediately

Howe realized he had spoken without considering a very

recent and very public example of union violence toward

those disagreeing with Osama's embrace of Ivan Stylin and

his commitment to support WOWU.

Bill Smiley was like a cat playing with a mouse. "Have

you personally, Howe, recently seen a prime example of

why secret ballots are necessary to avoid union violence?'

Howe's lip quivered involuntarily. "The accused are

innocent until proven guilty, Bill. Even union members."

Bill stuck the knife deep into Howe's facade. "Howe, didn't

you see the hundreds of replays on TV where several

WOWU members recently beat and brutally kicked a man

in St. Louis for simply appearing to disagree with them at a

town hall meeting promoting socialist agendas?"

Howe feigned a relaxed look. "It is yet to be proven

whether those carrying out such violence were actually

WOWU members or right wing rednecks masquerading as

union thugs." Bill cackled. "Their necks were black,

Howe. Just like your candidate's heart. Let's move on to the

issue of teaching a scientifically impossible conglom-

eration of alleged facts in our public schools in support of

the premise that God does not exist. What is your position,

Howe, on the theory of evolution? Do you believe that you,

Howe Snicker, are the result of trillions of random chance

events and mutational aberrations over billions of years

devoid of any design or purpose whatsoever?"

Howe again tried to confuse facts with imagination. "I

am not aware that the theory of evolution has been proven

to be impossible. Creation science has not demonstrated

any evolutionary explanation to be scientifically

unfounded."

Bill tried not to display his contempt for Howe's hypoc-

risy. "Howe, where have you been since Albert Einstein,

Robert Oppenheimer, Enrico Fermi, Edward Teller, I.I.

Rabi, Otto Hahn, Fritz Strassmann, Leo Szilard, and Lord

Rutherford demonstrated through the development of

nuclear weapons that energy holds matter together; that the

molecular structure of atomic particles is incredibly

complex and displays an irreducible level of complexity

which absolutely precludes random chance."

"Bill, you're talking about elements and their inherent

energy. Evolution deals with the origin of living organisms.

Bill was dumbfounded at Howe's rebuttal. "Howie, living

organisms are precise configurations of the basic elements

and are incapable of exhibiting life until the molecular

structure is transformed by creative energy. The single

celled bacterium E. coli, one of the simplest of life forms,

contains a predetermined balance of adenine, thymine,

guanine and cytosine nucleic acids arranged in four million

precise sequences. Only by copying its genetic code can E.

coli divide into two E. coli cells every twenty minutes. The

genetic code for every bacterium including E. coli had to

exist before the first bacterium appeared on Earth."

Cold logic never fazed Howe's mindset to believe

humans evolved from lower life forms. "The first genetic

code could have created itself by random chance." Bill

looked at him with unbridled astonishment. "Howe, do you

know how many electrons exist in our entire universe?"

Howie winced. "I believe I read somewhere that total

electron population lies somewhere between ten to the

fiftieth power and ten to the eightieth power."

"Excellent starting point, Howe. To illustrate the absolute

impossibility of the theory of evolution, consider that the

probability of predicting accurately the occurrence of twenty-five specific unrelated events is less than one chance in one thousand trillion trillion. For fifty-three specific unrelated events the chances of predicting all of them accurately is less than one chance in ten to the one hundred and fifty-seventh power."

Howie chuckled and maintained a smile. "I'll concede that is a rather large number and such a probability is somewhat unlikely." "Somewhat!!" Bill nearly choked. "It takes 2.5 times ten to the fifteenth power electrons laid side by side to make a single line of electrons one inch long. Just to count that inch of electrons at the rate of four per second would take nineteen million years counting continuously. Howie, if we had 10 to the one hundred and fifty-seventh power electrons, and we could fashion 500 balls of electrons six billion light years in radius, it would take six hundred million trillion years to use up our supply

of electrons." Bill spoke slowly to emphasize the
impossibility of his next point:

"Now, suppose only one of those electrons had a totally
unique atomic mark on it, and we shoot you into space. Do
you believe you could find that specific electron on your
first pick?"

Howe looked stumped. "It would be a long shot. What's
your point?"

"Actually, Howe, I am making three related points by
comparison. First, we have been mathematically describing the probability of correctly predicting fifty-three future
unrelated events. To randomly evolve the DNA code for E.
coli would require "mother nature" to correctly predict
four million precise sequences of DNA pairs of nucleic
acids, which is comparable to correctly guessing four
million lotto numbers. Since E. coli is a bacterium, the
simplest form of single-celled organisms, the DNA code

for E. coli had to exist before E. coli could begin to

multiply through simple cell division. Thus, Howie, we are

really comparing mathematical odds in terms of correctly

guessing 53 lotto numbers as opposed to 4,000,000 lotto

numbers (10 to the hundred and fifty-seventh power versus

10 x 4 to the millionth power). In view of these scientific

and mathematical facts, I ask you again, Howe: are you in

favor of teaching the totally ludicrous theory of evolution

in our public schools?"

Howe gave Bill a jaundiced look. "It is not my call. It's

the law." Bill jabbed his finger toward Howe. "Laws are

changed every session of Congress. Don't hide behind

outdated laws. Are you going to champion evolution

because Barry Osama has indicated he believes bacteria

evolved into humans?"

Howe played his last card. "Our constitution demands

separation between church and state. God and Jesus Christ

cannot be taught in our public schools." Bill laughed with scorn. "Did you study American history in Mombosa? Our founding fathers required the Bible to be used as a public school text book and conducted worship services in the Congress and the Supreme Court. How dare you suggest that America is not a Christian nation. Over three quarters of our population, even in the midst of abortion, infanticide, sexual perversion, and communistic government policies, profess to be God fearing Christians. Our federal constitution only forbids interference with religion or forcing Americans to worship according to a federal or state law mandate. If the handful of atheists in America are offended by our Christian heritage, they are certainly free to leave the country along with their offended children. I would suggest Saudi Arabia or Iran."

Howe thought about that for a second. "This is their native country. They have a right to be offended by something they do not believe in." Bill laughed with

amazement at Howie's moronic defense. "We are a

democracy, Howe. The will of the majority prevails in a

democracy and not judicial bias by judges abusing the

public trust. We, the majority, are deeply offended by the

pettiness of your tiny minority. We, the majority, pay for

public education. Therefore public education is whatever

we say it is. We are getting fed up with homosexuals,

abortionists and evolutionist legislating from the bench. Do

Barry Osama a personal favor and tell him not to offend us.

We will boot him back to Forenborn."

Bill took a deep breath. "We have to pause for a

commercial while I calm my nerves."

Barry Osama forked hot buttered lobster into his mouth

and kept his eyes glued on Timmy Notax. To maintain total

privacy, they were dining with Georgie Sorrow in a secure

conference room in Georgie's mansion. A trusted maid

served only when summoned by Georgie using a desig-

nated buzzer. All three men were dressed in slacks,

sweaters and comfortable slippers. Timmy nervously

nibbled at his salad. Timmy was forty-eight, average

height, blue eyed, slick black hair, oval face with smooth

skin, broad forehead, angular nose, and pointed chin. Some

people even considered him handsome.

Timmy's nervousness was prompted by major cheating

on his taxes to the tune of around $34,000. Barry and

Georgie had been considering him for Secretary of the

United States Treasury primarily because Timmy was a

criminal, liar, and thief and could be easily manipulated to

pilfer the public treasury. Barry dabbed his mouth with his

napkin and drank a little dinner wine. He grunted at Timmy

over the rim of his glass. "Your nomination will trigger

vetting by the Republicans including detailed auditing of

your tax returns for the last several years. How bad is it?"

Timmy stopped picking at his food and folded his hands

over his belly. "In the neighborhood of thirty-four grand."

"Peanuts!" Georgie snapped. "Volunteer the informa-

tion and blame the unintentional error on turbo tax and

your accountant. When the first thirty-four billion gets lost,

you may have to be more clever in covering our tracks."

"Don't sweat it, Timmy," Barry added. "We have already

decided you're the right man for these confusing and

troubled economic times. Hundreds of billions will be

flowing through very convoluted financial transactions and

you will be the one controlling where it ends up."

Georgie turned to Barry. "We have to do something

about Jojo Hiden making appearances on his own and

contradicting your statements, Barry. You better put him on

a shorter leash." "I'll take care of that problem," Barry

promised.

Glen Ripuone welcomed Nancy Tearieye and Barney
Smirk to his Telitright talk show. Glen, as usual, was
dressed causally and munched on M & M's. Nancy's face
was so drawn from cosmetic surgery that she had a tough
time trying to smile. She had perfected a wet eye look to
indicate her deep sympathy for oppressed aliens and
citizens without health insurance. She was dressed
carelessly and her cheek hugging, dyed brown hair
appeared windblown. Nancy reflected the image of an
aging floozie searching for the fountain of youth. In a
much earlier era she might have been considered
moderately attractive. Her high cheek bones and sloped
nose blended with thin lips and a strong chin. She shook
hands with Glen and made herself comfortable in a padded
arm chair.

Glen turned his attention to Barney who seemed to have

a perpetual sore throat. He wore a tweed suit that looked

slept in and a soiled white dress shirt adorned with a

sagging red tie. His white hair, chubby oval cheeks, pug

nose, dentures and thick glasses gave him a wino image.

Glen shook his hand like caressing a snake and seated

himself as Barney settled in next to Nancy. Glen forced

himself to smile at Nancy. "Presidential candidate Barry

Osama pledged more transparency and honesty in

governmental deliberations. Do you, Nancy, share Barry's

desire for no secret meetings, no back room bargaining,

and no surprising the American people with unconstitut-

ional laws and taxes buried in hundreds of pages of legal

bafflegab?"

Nancy tried to smile as much as she dared. "I share our

next president's view that all Congressional bills should be

openly debated and the details fully explained to

Americans before a floor vote is allowed. I would

moreover favor the taking of polls to ensure that a majority

of voters favor the legislation."

Glen nodded his approval. "Should you wind up in

January, 2009 with a Democratic super majority in

Congress and a liberal radical in the White House, will you

work in a bipartisan manner with Republicans?" Nancy

searched for a handkerchief in case her tears started

flowing. "The Republicans are destroying our economy

and threatening the future of all Americans. I personally

will invite them to join us in avoiding unsound fiscal

policy and protecting American jobs."

"What are your current plans, Nancy, for controlling

government spending and creating more American jobs?"

Nancy's eyes began watering. "Too many Americans are

dying in Iraq and Afghanistan. The Hush administration

squandered our precious resources and allowed the enemy

to regroup and rearm. We will accelerate the war to a

successful conclusion and bring our troops home. Ending

the Hush wars will save taxpayers more than a trillion

dollars and we will also eliminate wasteful Republican

pork barrel programs and Medicare fraud. Medicare fraud

is currently estimated at over five hundred billion which

means we will eliminate over one and a half trillion dollars

in wasteful spending."

Glen didn't change his facial expression. "That's very

encouraging, Nancy. What specifically will the liberal

Democrats do to accelerate the wars in Iraq and Afghan-

istan? Send more troops? Try to buy off more warlords?

More bombing and less ground action? Kill more terrorists

with less concern over civilian casualties? More training

for local police and military units? Blockade both

countries? Convince the UN to take over and fund the wars

to eliminate terrorism? What will you do that the Hush

administration has not attempted to do consistent with both

financial and humanitarian concerns?"

Nancy assumed her "third in succession" Commander-in-Chief posture. "We will force the Iraqis and the Afghans to shoulder the burden for their own security by setting a firm date of December 31, 2011 for bringing our troops home and to discontinue funding the Iraqi and Afghan security forces."

Glen looked completely bewildered. "Nancy, why are we fighting terrorists in Iraq and Afghanistan?" Nancy looked puzzled. "To stop terrorist attacks against the United States." Nancy set her jaw firmly indicating feminine resolve.

"Yes, of course," Glen replied. "Why didn't Barry Osama think of that. He wants to just negotiate with terrorists. The radical liberal strategy amounts to threatening impotent sanctions and assuring the terrorists that if they just hang in there until the end of 2011, they will win because that is our surrender date. That typifies

Harvard military strategy leavened with a heavy cocaine

sniffing schedule and world government ideology." Nancy

got teary eyed again. "We can't just keep killing Iraqi and

Afghan women and children. There has to be an end to

such carnage." She sniffed for effect and dabbed at her

eyes.

Glen was not impressed. "The concept of a humane war

was championed by progressives who are socialists and

communists hiding behind public ignorance of actual

human history. Populations who passively tolerate mad dog

killers have no logical reason to complain when those

being shielded are under attack. You live with terrorists,

you die with terrorists. That is the true history of warfare.

You cannot defeat an enemy in a foreign country protected

by the population without killing a large number of

civilians."

Nancy was horrified. "You would indiscriminately bomb the Iraqi and Afghan cities in order to kill the terrorists?" Glen reminded himself that Nancy did not graduate from West Point. "Not exactly indiscriminately, Nancy. The terrorists are cowards and suicidal Islamic extremists. They hide behind their women and children. They are incapable of logical, intelligent human compassion. We have to kill them. Shall we kill them in their home countries or in New York, California, Washington, DC, Newark and Milwaukee, or perhaps in every American city they freely target? No, Nancy. We force their hand. We drop leaflets over those areas sheltering terrorist strongholds warning civilians to leave while a couple of battalions encircle the stronghold and weed out enemy combatants during the civilian exodus. Then we bomb that city, town, village, hamlet or mountainous region into very small fragments of terrorists and sheltering structures. Since the terrorists believe

suicide missions send them straight to Paradise to copulate

eternally with seventy-two brown eyed virgins, we

eliminate their incentive to randomly murder innocent

people. We faithfully castrate every terrorist killed and

bury them in mass graves filled with pig fat. Thereby, the

seventy-two virgins incentive is mooted and the mad dog

killer is denied entry into Paradise because Allah won't

tolerate those defiled with pig fat." Glen eyed Nancy with

partially concealed mirth.

"The terrorist leaders and clerics we hang from the

surviving trees and pour boiling pig fat over their Muslim

corpses. In this manner, Nancy, we clue the world in that

we Americans will not tolerate terrorists attacking us under

any circumstances. That we, in fact, will kill them without

blinking an eye and send them castrated and defiled with

pig fat directly to their eternal habitat." Nancy turned a

little green and Glen moved on to the issue of illegal aliens:

"You have stated, Nancy, that you favor amnesty for

illegal aliens and a streamlined process for full citizenship.

That would obviously include food stamps, health care,

rent subsidies, section eight housing, aid for dependent

children, student aid, and various other government

freebies. Do you anticipate, Nancy, that granting amnesty

and proving nanny government programs to perhaps

twenty million more illegal aliens might result in a

perpetual Democratic voting majority? Our presidential

elections are usually determined by less than a five million

vote spread. Is amnesty for illegal aliens a clever vote

buying scheme?"

Nancy squealed: "Are you kidding?!! Are you kidding?!!

Glen smiled back at her. "No, Nancy. I am deadly serious

and I think your scheme is quite transparent. Tell me. Since

you are not paying health insurance for the illegal aliens

working in your vineyards, what happens when one of the

wetbacks laboring in your Napa Valley properties needs

emergency medical treatment?"

Nancy became visually flustered. "An ambulance is

called and the individual is taken directly to the nearest

emergency room for treatment." Glen raised his eyebrows.

"Who pays the bill for such medical treatment?" Nancy

dabbed at her moist eyes. "If the worker is unable to pay

for emergency treatment the government picks up the tab

and the bill is paid by the appropriate federally funded

entity."

Glen looked offended. "In that case, Nancy, why do we

need to disrupt the finest healthcare system in the world to

force feed a nationalized healthcare flimflam to provide

healthcare insurance for people who are already getting

quality health care for free? I have never seen anyone

dying in our streets for lack of healthcare insurance. What

is the big emergency? If we can provide free healthcare for
illegal aliens we can certainly do the same for our legal
citizens who do not earn enough to pay health insurance
premiums. And, in fact, we are doing so now. People with
attachable assets between jobs and those not covered while
employed by a company not providing health insurance can
be covered without nationalizing our healthcare. We don't
have to penalize the overwhelming majority to provide
nanny healthcare for the fourteen percent minority."

Nancy mimicked a stop sign. "Don't forget, Glen, that
we plan to reduce cost by reducing waste, eliminating
Medicare and Medicaid fraud and lowering procedural
expenses."   Glen rocked back and laughed softly. "Nancy,
we don't need nationalized healthcare to address Medicare
and Medicaid fraud. We just need to enforce existing laws.
Government has never, ever, eliminated any waste to my
knowledge. The government has never done anything with

less cost or more efficiently than the private sector. The

free market has proven again and again that the govern-

ment is wasteful, disorganized, inept, corrupt, and

dishonest." Glen smiled and handed Nancy a fresh

handkerchief, then tossed down a couple of M & M's.

"The biggest liars in our society are members of

Congress and presidential candidates. Your radically

liberal, socialistic healthcare takeover will create a shortage

of doctors, bankrupt numerous hospitals, and retard new

drug research. Many physicians will refuse to treat

Medicare patients. Timely medical treatment will become

impossible to provide and senior citizens will be denied

routine and necessary medical procedures. How do you

plan to ration healthcare between welfare recipients and

senior citizens? Will you sacrifice the elderly in favor of

those who are able to work but do not want a job?"

Nancy blinked back tears. "We want everyone to have

quality and timely health care. We will not favor one

category of citizens over another." Glen exhibited both

patience and tolerance for utter nonsense.

"Nancy, who is going to pay for all this government

bureaucracy and healthcare chaos without skyrocketing

taxes and a quagmire of red tape. I understand the rough

draft of your proposed socialistic takeover of healthcare

covers more than a thousand pages of legal mumble

jumble. Why is this bill not being openly debated and the

precise provisions made public?"

Nancy again conjured up her moist eye routine. "We

need to finalize this healthcare bill and push it through to

relieve the pain and suffering of the people currently being

denied medical treatment. The Republicans are just being

obstructionists." Glen looked confused. "There is no one

in America being denied life saving medical treatment.

What is the midnight emergency, Nancy? What are you

hiding by keeping the public ignorant of the details of this
bill while it is being rushed to a vote virtually in secret?"

Nancy pretended to be surprised by Glen's question.
"My door is always open to Republicans as well as
Democrats. I welcome bipartisan participation."

Glen glanced toward the cameras. "We'll be right back
after a commercial break to talk with Barney Smirk about
the bankruptcy of the United States." During commercials,
Glen reviewed his notes on gross national product for the
United States and the European Union as a percentage of
total global wealth.

When the last commercial faded, he turned to Barney
Smirk. "Barney, as Chairman of the House Financial
Services Committee overseeing securities, insurance,
banking and housing industries, can you tell us whether the
United States is now bankrupt?" Barney gave Glen his
best homosexual profile.

"Bankrupt is an ambiguous term and is applied to many situations inappropriately." Glen did not take the bait for changing the subject. "Barney, I am asking you whether the United States' current debt exceeds our total national wealth. Do we owe more than we can pay?" Barney pursed his swollen lips. "Not as long as other nations will buy our bonds. The world's economies are still indexed to the dollar."

"Barney, what happens if our creditor nations begin dumping their inventory of dollars due to declining value of U.S. currency? The dollar is down thirty percent in global currency markets since 2002. Americans on fixed incomes have lost nearly a third of their purchasing power. This also means that the dollar inventory of our creditor nations is also worth thirty percent less. As our dollar continues to decline in value, how long will the healthy economies around the world continue to measure their wealth in U.S. currency?"

Barney's background was law not finance. He answered

with the same ignorance that nourished his political

agenda. "We are the largest customer of our largest

creditors. If their economic policies dry up our demand for

their goods and services they cut their own throats."

Glen again laughed inwardly. "Barney, let's pretend I'd

like to buy your home which you'd like to sell. Let's also

pretend the fair market value of your home in 2002 was

one million U.S. dollars. I am willing to pay you one

million dollars for your property. A British executive

transferred to the U.S. is willing to pay you one million

British pounds as indexed to the Euro. Would you take a

thirty percent loss on your home in order to sell to me?

Now, suppose the dollar falls another thirty percent against

the Euro which is increasing in value. Would you take a

sixty percent loss on your home in order to sell to me?

Now, further suppose the United States wants to borrow

against U.S. bonds five hundred billion dollars from China

to whom we already owe roughly a trillion dollars.

However, China is terrified by U.S. runaway printing of

dollars with nothing guaranteeing the value of the dollar

but more U.S. borrowing. Consequently, China decides to

convert its inventory of dollars to Euros to avoid further

dollar losses. China still wants to sell to the U.S. so China

is willing to buy U.S. bonds at a higher interest rate so we

can spend a trillion dollars on your communist healthcare

takeover. If the dollar is indexed to the Euro we have to

pay back the one trillion plus the devaluation of 60% plus

the agreed upon interest rate." Glen glowered at Barney.

"Now, due to such insane debt escalation, the dollar

falls another twenty-five percent against the Euro. The

dollar is now worth fifteen percent of its 2002 value.

Eighty-five to ninety percent of the wealth of the United

States as measured by our creditors has now disappeared

since 2002. In view of this almost certain scenario,

Barney, as Chairman of the House Financial Services

Committee overseeing securities, banking, insurance and

housing, would you consider America bankrupt?"

It was painfully obvious that Barney was incapable of

comprehending elementary economics. His answer was

another ambiguous dodge. "The collapse of the U.S.

economy would cause a domino effect around the globe.

The United States is simply too big to fail. The world

cannot cope with the fallout from the disintegration of the

American economy."

Glen tried a different approach to help Barney under-

stand that the radical liberal Democrats manipulating him

were intentionally bankrupting the United States to usher in

a global government.

"Barney, the value of all goods and services produced

by the combined economies of the entire world calculates

to slightly under seventy trillion dollars not adjusted for

continued deflation of U.S. currency. Our current debt

exceeds thirteen trillion. Our unfunded debt to provide

existing entitlement programs such as Medicare, Medicaid,

social security, and miscellaneous welfare programs equals

another ninety-six trillion. In other words, Barney, we

currently have compiled a total debt more than fifty percent

greater than the annual gross national product of the entire

world. And, Barney, your scheming communist cohorts are

still writing Congressional bills for more trillion dollar

entitlement programs. It appears, Mr. Chairman, that the

communists have taken over our government and loaded us

onto a fast train headed for a one world government ruled

by a deluded dictator."

Barney, being a radical liberal, never really thought

much about the debt he helped create. "We intend, Mr.

Ripuone, to sweep up after President Hush's failed policies

by creating more jobs, lowering taxes on the working class

and ensuring that every citizen has access to quality

healthcare."

"How are you going to accomplish those admirable

objectives, Barney. Perhaps eat more fast food? Less than

ten percent of Americans are employed producing an

exportable product. That is because we are no longer

competitive in the world market. One of our remaining

capital goods industries is motor vehicles. You and your

fellow communists are propping up an industrial corpse

with taxpayer money. Unions like WOWU have priced

American labor out of the global market. Outside of

agriculture, over eighty percent of American workers are

employed in service related jobs which only support our

domestic needs. We have nothing to export. Certainly the

emerging industrial nations will not want our financial

advice or educational system which produces high school graduates who cannot read. Where is all this great society money coming from, Barney? Our only option is more debt and more deflation of our currency."

Barney appeared more relaxed. "Sounds like you are making a logical case for a one world government where all workers will receive fair and equitable compensation for doing the same job. I can support that equality." Glen did not smile. "You mean the utopia enjoyed by the Russians, and the Chinese, and the Cubans; and every other nation which now wants to convert from communism to capitalism. Socialism and communism will not work for any extended period because of basic human nature. Only capitalism produces individual freedom to succeed or fail economically." Barney voiced no rebuttal allowing Glen to finish his point:

"Socialism and communism consistently degenerate into

a mediocre and crumbling human society due to lack of

individual incentive. Such utopian forms of government

exist only in the minds of deluded politicians. How many

times, Barney, must you be proven wrong before you stop

trying to destroy the most successful government that has

ever existed?   Glen cut off any reply from Barney. "We'll

be back after a short commercial break to meet our next

guest, Treasury Secretary Heiny Takmore."

Barry Osama and Jojo Hiden worked the Democrats

gathered in Dayton, Ohio into a frenzy. WOWU jackets

and banners were abundant.

"Change!!" Barry shouted. "Change from the eight years

of Republican stagnation. Change from the failed Hush

economic policies. Change from unemployment lines to

booming factories. Change from wasting tens of billions on

never ending wars to funding education and healthcare for

low income families. Change for the oppressed minorities

from poverty to ladders of opportunity. Change you can

believe in. Change is what you will get from my admini-

stration!!"

Barry and Jojo smiled and waved and smiled and

waved.

Jojo took up the cudgel to hammer foreign policy. His

false teeth flashed in the morning sunlight.

"Change!! Change from a policy of military intervention

to more productive negotiations. Change from meddling in

the affairs of other nations to managing our problems at

home. Change from back breaking military budgets to

better education and standard of living for working

Americans. Change you can count on!! Change you can

believe in!! We're bringing change to Washington. Get out

and vote!!! We need your help!!"

Barry and Jojo smiled and waved and smiled and

waved.

The commercial faded and Glen welcomed Heiny Takmore to a guest chair. Heiny's bald head was damp from nervous tension. He was dressed like a wall street tycoon manicured to perfection. His charcoal gray suit blended pleasingly with white silk shirt, gray striped tie and double polished black leather shoes.

Heiny was tall and muscular with nicely balanced features and square chin. He had recently celebrated his sixty-third birthday and looked like a bald and elderly Christopher Reeves.

Glen's zip-up boots, dress jeans and blue pullover sweater contrasted sharply with Heiny's Brooks Brothers outfit. Glen shook Heiny's hand and Heiny sat down trying very hard to appear relaxed. Glen eyed him with puzzle-ment.

"Heiny, since the auto makers and the unions have

pursued a strategy that has made U.S. automobiles

uncompetitive in the world market, why do you favor

keeping them out of bankruptcy court for a couple more

years using taxpayer money? Why not simply let the free

market weed out such poorly managed business enterprises

and unions thereby giving other Americans a chance to

produce quality cars that can compete with foreign auto

makers?"

Compound questions always intimidated Heiny. He

resorted to job loss justification. "The auto makers employ

thousands of workers and during a severe economic

downturn we simply cannot allow them to go under."

"They've already gone under, Heiny. The doors just haven't

been shut yet. The unions won't make any major conces-

sions and the companies cannot continue dumping billions

of dollars into a bottomless pit. Assembly line workers in

auto plants are compensated like they are lawyers and

doctors; like motivated individuals who have invested

fifteen to twenty years getting a professional education plus

a quarter of a million or so in tuition, room and board."

Glen reached for his M & M's and offered Heiny some.

"Auto assembly line workers, on the other hand, are one

notch above trained chimpanzees. Not many people will

buy American cars loaded with ridiculous labor costs when

foreign cars are readily available produced with equitable

labor allocation. The U.S. auto makers and the unions

bargained like only Americans make and sell automobiles.

The existing American auto industry is dead and will

eventually be buried regardless of how much taxpayer

money you squander. Products burdened with disproportio-

nate labor costs will be rejected by the world market in

which we must compete. Do you have some secret plan to

save the U.S. auto makers, Heiny?"

Heiny looked somewhat flustered. He knew Glen was

well informed and would jump on a political slogan. "We

believe it is appropriate to give the auto makers and the

unions a limited time to address the inequity issues. At

some point, the government will have to intervene on

behalf of the American economy. If a solution cannot be

agreed upon between the auto makers and the unions, the

bailout will be discontinued and the bankruptcy courts will

oversee the disposition of salvageable assets and the free

market will reinvent the American automotive industry.

The stockholders of Ford, Chrysler and General Motors

will lose a few billions but such is the nature of capitalism.

In the meanwhile, hundreds of thousands will join the

unemployment ranks. The recession will deepen and

recovery will be retarded. Nonetheless, we have weathered

much worse economic disasters and we will survive this

one also."

"Well stated, Heiny. If left alone the free market will

eventually stabilize our economy. The problem that we

now face is that maniacal government spending has

bankrupted the United States and we may well have passed

the point of no return. There is no possibility that we can

over the short term pay our debts. If our creditors liquidate

their dollar inventories our currency will become virtually

worthless and our economy will disintegrate. It is not

possible under any form of government whether

democratic, socialist or communist to spend trillions that

require future massive taxation over several generations.

First, our creditors will not keep holding on to dollars that

keep decreasing in value. Second, our current economic

woes would only be passed on to future American

generations during an extended depression that would

dwarf the Hoover and FDR madness. Third, Americans

will not stand for such oppression by political demagogues.

There would be a bloody revolution in this nation that

would result in the elimination of greedy, lying, forked

tongued politicians."

Heiny did not respond and Glen became more

aggressive. "We still have our guns, Heiny. Our founding

fathers correctly foresaw the need for an armed population

to fend off oppressive government and massive poverty.

Also, don't forget that our armed forces are controlled by

military officers who are not radical liberal Democrats.

When the masses face starvation, our military forces will

behave just like the Russian military did during the fall of

the Soviet Union. We will not tolerate imbecilic domestic

and foreign policy indefinitely. Go visit the mass graves in

Ghana where the political pigs are buried if you doubt what

the future holds. The only happenstance that prevented a

revolution during the Hoover and Roosevelt years was

World War II which triggered a massive war machine in

America with full employment and hundreds of thousands

transferred from soup lines to the battlefield."

Heiny was totally dumbfounded. He squinted at a

fearless American on world television that would speak the

truth regardless of the consequences. "Do you have a

solution to the problems you have summarized?"

Glen did not blink. "Yes. Stop spending trillions that do

not exist in our national treasury. Let the greedy, insolent

auto workers join the ranks of the unemployed. Let the

bankruptcy courts liquidate the auto makers and distribute

the salvaged monies in accordance with existing bank-

ruptcy laws. Notify our creditors that we have shut down

our money presses and will pay our existing debts over a

ten year period. Pass laws requiring balanced state and

federal budgets. Discontinue all welfare programs and any

public assistance that will encourage foreign aliens to

violate our borders. Discontinue all subsidies and all other

forms of welfare to able bodied men and women under the

age of sixty-seven. Use our welfare reserves to rebuild our state and federal infrastructure. Utilize our oil reserves located under our public lands and our offshore waters regardless of location. Discontinue all foreign aid of any type and put the funds into Medicare and Medicaid reserves. Build an infrastructure for utilizing methane, propane, natural gas, oxygen, and hydrogen as alternate energy sources. Restructure income tax to be a flat rate of fifteen percent with zero tax deductions. Replace coal fired power plants with nuclear facilities. Maintain a backlog of projects to strengthen and beautify America thereby eliminating unemployment and providing jobs for those who want to work." Glen paused, but Heiny chose not to reply. Glen charged forward.

"These projects would be funded by reserves for unemployment benefits and elimination of the attending bureaucracy which produce nothing in return for funds expended. Maintain a vigilant system to round up and

deport all foreigners who enter the country illegally.

Reduce Congressional salaries and benefits by sixty

percent. Fix the Presidential and White House budget at

fifty percent of what is is now. Institute maximum prison

sentences for any public servant who violates state or

federal penal codes. In this manner, Heiny, we pay our

debts, eliminate unemployment and send public servants to

Washington who truly want to serve rather than rip off

American citizens. We also maintain a reliable infra-

structure and beautify our country."

Glen sorted through his notes. "Now, Heiny, lets talk

about bailing out mega financial institutions and their

executives who raked in hundreds of millions while

bankrupting their organizations. You championed these

monolithic bailouts after taking enormous bonuses while

Chairman and Chief Executive officer of Goldbars and

Upayus. Can you explain this business and financial logic

to me?"

Heiny revealed his true hypocrisy. "I earned those

bonuses by making intelligent, well reasoned decisions as

CEO of one of the most successful investment banking

firms in America. Thus, I do not apologize for the financial

return on my successful management of Goldbars and

Upayus. As for the bailouts of major financial institutions,

it was simply to the government's advantage to loan money

to these conglomerates to cope with the financial crisis

Congressional blunders created. The bailouts saved the

economy from further chaos."

Glen smiled with restrained anger. "I see, Heiny. But,

just for my viewers' benefit, let me clear up what I just

heard. Goldbars and Upayus made a fantastic killing in the

free market by taking huge risks hoping for a big return.

The risks paid off and you personally made half a billion

dollars while the taxpayers sweated in factories and service

jobs. Then, when Goldbars and Upayus plus several other

financial conglomerates made some bad decisions and lost

their ass, you, as Secretary of the U.S. Treasury, felt it

timely and appropriate that the taxpayers finance the

recovery of Goldbars and Upayus and other multi-billion

dollar firms. And, just to demonstrate your undying

gratitude for the taxpayers bailing out major banking

organizations, you twiddled your thumbs while the

taxpayers' money was used to pay enormous management

bonuses and throw lavish parties at luxury resorts instead

of extending loans to small business to help turn the

economy around. Those three hundred million dollar

salaries and billions of dollars in bonuses most certainly

saved the economy from further chaos. Isn't that a fair

restatement of your intelligent, well reasoned decisions as

Secretary of the United States Treasury, Heiny?"

"The government loaned the money, Glen. It was not a donation in any sense of the word. The major banks paid the salaries and bonuses to keep their executive management staff."

Glen bit his tongue and remained civil. "Heiny, your justification for risking the taxpayers' money without any taxpayer approval was to keep the flow of credit moving within the economy. The banks were facing bankruptcy. They could not qualify for multi-billion dollar loans. You told the taxpayers that if the banks did not get the taxpayer loans the economy would collapse. Had you been honest and told the American public that their money was being loaned to pay exorbitant salaries and ridiculous bonuses to the ignoramuses who bankrupted their own organizations, I believe there would have been rioting in the streets."

Jim McPaign and Sarah Planke warmed to the huge

crowd in St. Louis. Being a swing state, Missouri was

evenly divided between Republicans and Democrats. The

Democrats tended to be jammed into the large urban areas.

The middle class suburbs, farms and scattered rural towns

were heavily Republican. The Republicans paid hefty taxes

and the Democrats, except for the few elite liberals, either

paid a minimum tax or no income tax at all. Between forty

and fifty percent of Democrats were getting food stamps,

Medicaid, unemployment benefits, aid to dependent

children, SSI and miscellaneous other government freebies.

Barry Osama had promised them even more handouts by a

new tax on the capitalists providing American jobs.

Jim and Sarah stood on a temporary platform and were

leading the crowd in "God Bless America." Both candi-

dates held microphones close to their lips and sang lustily.

Following the last verse, Jim and Sarah smiled and waved

while the crowd cheered and clapped.

Jim took a couple of steps forward and addressed the gathering. "Thank you!! Thank you!! It's a pleasure to be in Missouri and especially so in St. Louis. Your arch and park grounds are even lovelier than they appear on TV. We're expecting to see the St. Louis Cardinals in the upcoming World Series."

The crowd shrieked with enthusiasm. Jim waited until the noise abated, then spoke directly into his microphone. "The election is fast approaching and we need your support as well as your votes. We're fully committed to lower taxes, to less government interference with the free market, and to sending corrupt officials to the unemployment lines." The crowd clapped and cheered, then let Jim continue:

"We'll make job creation the number one public priority. But, we need your help. Nearly half of our American citizens are living off your tax dollars and don't want a job because they can draw more welfare than the jobs pay for which they are qualified. Why is this? It is because less

than one third of Americans have a college education.

Therefore two thirds of our total population are only

qualified for factory and assembly line work and minimum

wage service jobs. Those with secretarial and computer

skills can earn a a little more. Beginning with the Franklin

D. Roosevelt administration, Progressives and Liberals

have been levying taxes on you to encourage people not to

work who haven't bothered to get an education. While you

work and pay heavy taxes, pimps, whores, crackheads, and

other able bodied welfare sponges are getting your tax

dollars. Your tax dollars are being squandered in the form

of numerous welfare programs that began with FDR and

have been expanded under each Democratic administration

over the last seventy years."

"Throw the bums out!! Throw the bums out!!"

chanted the listeners. When the noise abated, Jim

continued: "Taxpayer funded assistance for handicapped

and disabled citizens is necessary and must continue.

However, the welfare and entitlement programs that

encourage uneducated, able bodied men and women not to

work are picking your pockets and transforming America

into a beggar nation. Democrats keep telling the willingly

uneducated that they are being oppressed and exploited and

are therefore entitled to full government support at the

expense of those paying taxes. Democrats also favor open

borders for illegal aliens to cross and become wards of the

government. By treating illegal aliens like American

citizens, the Democrats are simply buying votes to stay in

control of every aspect of your life as hard working

taxpaying citizens."

Again, the crowd vented: "Throw the bums out!!

Throw the bums out!!" Jim paused and patiently waited to

be heard. Sarah smiled and waved. The chanting petered

out and Jim continued:

"The math is not complicated. Beginning with FDR and continuing until today, the Democrats have reduced roughly half of all Americans to dependence upon welfare in one form or another. By giving illegal aliens citizenship status and eligibility to vote, the Democrats are in the very near future going to have a voting majority of citizens on welfare plus illegal aliens converted to government dependent citizens. America will be transformed from a free Democratic republic to a socialist society where everyone will be equally poor and hungry. This is what Osama means by "transforming America." Radical liberal Democrats have been working toward this transformation since the Thomas Woodrow Wilson administration. The undercover communists currently wearing the masks of progressives, liberals and socialists will become highly visible and in control of government when America falls due to treason from within."

The crowd became quiet and very attentive to Jim McPaign which allowed him to finish his address without distracting noise and applause.

"A great nation may survive the truly ignorant, the greedy, the lazy, the shiftless, and self-proclaimed intellectuals; but seldom will it survive treason from within itself. Internal treason is a slow growing cancer that suddenly blooms when given the opportunity to kill its victim. The radical liberal Democrats think that getting Barry Osama elected President of the United States will finish off the last remaining superpower by reinventing America in the image of socialist nations. But, why would any patriotic American want to become another Soviet Union? The Russian people finally revolted to throw off the yoke of socialism. There is not a remaining socialist nation in existence today whose population does not want to be like Americans and enjoy a free, democratic and

capitalistic society. So, why are super rich radical

Democrats like Georgie Sorrow spending close to a billion

dollars to get Osama elected? The answer is power. They

want to be the Alexander the Great that succeeded rather

than died in a drunker stupor. They want to dictate their

beliefs into laws humans must live by. They know

socialism and communism have never succeeded for any

period of time. They just are convinced they are so much

smarter than the rest of us and can thus succeed where

everyone else has failed. They are ego maniacs who will

destroy the spirit and soul of America to enjoy self-

worship. Therefore, I say to you, choose in this

presidential election whom you believe will serve you

instead of a lost socialistic cause. Let's turn back the clock

to when we still taught American history in our public

schools and a student had to demonstrate a full

understanding of our federal constitution. Let's go back to

when we taught our children how equality, opportunity and

capitalism made possible life, liberty and the pursuit of

happiness."

A thunderous roar echoed through the streets of

downtown St. Louis. The cheering, applause, whistling and

foot stamping went on for a full five minutes until Sarah

Planke finally stopped smiling and waving and began

speaking into her microphone. The people quieted down to

hear Sarah.

"We know we are not going to get the votes of those

dependent upon a nanny government. We are not appealing

to the surrogate children of radical liberal Democrats. This

is not a question of race. There are more white Americans

on welfare than any other nationality. It is time to speak

very clearly about what the Democrats are up to. They

have created an ongoing voting block of welfare recipients

and citizens who must depend on entitlement programs

funded by taxpayers. Nearly half of our citizens pay no

income tax and will vote for Democrats to keep getting the

freebies. Once Democrats are successful in attracting

another ten to fifteen million illegal aliens through our

back door and putting them on our government dole and

helping them register to vote, the two party system will

cease to exist. The Democrats will have achieved a voting

block representing more than fifty percent of our voting

population." Sarah raised her fist.

"This must not happen because in four years the

socialists and communists hiding under the label of liberals

will have the total control they need to convert America

into a beggar nation. We are not against immigrants

coming to this country. We support lawful immigration and

legally obtained citizenship. We are totally against criminal

crossing of our borders and voting by non-citizens. We

must stop the Democrats now before they obtain an

irreversible voting majority. We are asking hard working,

tax paying Americans to give us a chance to clean up

Washington and return to a government of the people, by

the people and for the people."

Again, the crowd screamed their agreement and vented

their emotions. Jim addressed the crowd again. "Allan

Snowyew and Jerry Jerksome are raking in millions on the

talk show circuit and solicitations by conning the public

about global warming. Snowyew and Jerksome warn us

the oceans will rise two feet in a few years flooding the

planet. The polar bears will die off. There will be massive

flooding and famine. In the near future the human race will

starve. Nations are in panic and calling emergency meeting

to address short term extinction. I want your close attention

while I read an article published about global warming:

'The Arctic ocean is warming up, icebergs are growing

scarcer and in some places the seals are finding the water

too hot, according to a report to the Commerce Department

yesterday from Consul Ifft, at Bergen, Norway. Reports

from fishermen, seal hunters and explorers, he declared, all

point to a radical change in climate conditions and hitherto

unheard-of temperatures in the Arctic zone. Exploration

expeditions report that scarcely any ice has been met with

as far north as 81 degrees 29 minutes. Soundings to a depth

of 3,100 meters showed the gulf stream still very warm.

Great masses of ice have been replaced by moraines of

earth and stones, the report continued, while at many points

well-known glaciers have entirely disappeared. Very few

seals and no white fish are found in the eastern Arctic,

while vast shoals of herring and smelts, which have never

before ventured so far north, are being encountered in the

old seal-fishing grounds. The article further states that if

the conditions continue, we will all be doomed in 20 years

or less because the entire earth will be covered by water
from the melting ice. The report gave no reason for the
global warming.'

"Oh, by the way . . . . . I'm sorry. I neglected to
mention that this report was from November 2, 1922 as
reported by the Associated Press and published in the
Washington Post."

Barry Osama, Jojo Hiden, Timmy Notax, and Derick
Loser were enjoying Georgie Sorrow's mansion and
attending servants. They nibbled on caviar with exotic
crackers and sipped fine champagne. Georgie voiced his
concern over a possible outbreak of violence when the U.S.
economy disintegrates:

"Some street violence is very probable and might
spread into a full blown revolution. We must have a
contingency plan." "I agree," Barry stated flatly. "The

rednecks can keep their Bibles but we must get their guns.

Since we will be in total control of Congress and the White

House, we can easily pass a law outlawing private owner-

ship of firearms. The problem I see is collection of millions

of weapons after the law takes effect. What do you suggest

Derick? As U.S. Attorney General, the responsibility of

collection will fall upon you."

Derick pursed his lips thoughtfully. "I have given the

matter considerable thought and I believe we can avoid

massive resistance by announcing that immediate

collection of illegal arms is necessary to avoid further mass

killings by rednecks and anarchists opposing legally

constituted authority. The media can help lower resistance

by pointing out that illegal firearms possession is now a

felony that would justify temporary confinement in a

holding area awaiting formal trial. In order to post bond the

detainee would have to surrender all firearms and

ammunition. The media can also point out that there will

be millions of rabid gun owners who will defy the law and

keep their weapons. To address the detainment in mass

logistics, we can use the existing interment camps scattered

around the country which can accommodate up to forty

million detainees."

Jojo Hiden was ecstatic. "Hell yes!! That will work

with no problem once the media makes the camps public.

The threat of being locked up in a holding camp will throw

a scare into most gun owners. The rest we can handle on an

individual basis. Derick can start working on the necessary

details now."

Georgie nodded with approval. "That will work out

once we have the reins of government."

Timmy Notax was anxious to contribute. "The

population is roughly split on the gun control issue. Both

sides have some serious activists. We can offer a reward for information leading to the arrest of those refusing to turn in their firearms and ammunition. Better yet, we can offer to buy the guns at fair market value to provide an incentive to voluntarily comply with the law."

Georgie signaled the waiter for more caviar and champagne. "I'll drink to that."

Willie Watchem greeted Senator Joe Debatem with a cordial smile and firm handshake. "Welcome to the show, Senator. It's nice to have you back to tell us what's going on in Washington."

Joe sat down in an armchair across from Willie. After twenty-two years in the Senate, he was well connected. He presented the astute politician image with closely cropped white hair, blue eyes and handsome features. He managed his weight well for his short height. He wore a tailored black suit with pink shirt and gray tie.

"I appreciate the invitation and the opportunity to address your viewers. The election is now three days away and I want the American people to know exactly where I stand on the key issues such as nationalized healthcare and illegal immigration. I also want to express my opposition to bailing out incompetent bankers and the stimulus package."

Willie gave Joe an affirmative nod. "Let's start with illegal immigration. Do you suspect some vote buying connected with amnesty for illegal aliens?"

"I most certainly do, Willie. Why else would the Democrats encourage aliens to break our laws. Our arms are always open to legal immigrants. From time to time it is necessary to restrict a massive influx of immigrants but the United States favors legal immigration. Those aliens coming in our front door rather than sneaking across our borders generally become productive, tax paying, law abiding and responsible citizens and therefore do not

depend upon welfare. Neither do they form a dependable

voting block for government freebies associated with

liberal Democrats. The Democrats want the millions of

illegal aliens that disregard our laws and sneak into the

United States to be welfare recipients and dependent upon

taxpayer subsidies. The illegal aliens are quickly educated

by community organizers that the Democrats will keep the

freebies flowing their way."

"Do you recommend giving citizenship status and thus

the vote to the twenty million or so illegal aliens that are

inside our borders now?"

"Absolutely not. Why have immigration laws if we do

not enforce them. Giving these criminals citizenship status

is like telling a burglar he can keep the TV he stole out of

your house. There are twin evils at work in the Democrat's

vote buying strategy. First, they are encouraging criminal

trespass. Second, they are circumventing our citizenship requirements and dumping another onerous burden on law abiding taxpayers. They know the illegal aliens will become life long and devout Democrats."

Willie asked a related question: "Do you think the illegal aliens already here should receive free health care?"

"No, for similar reasons. Healthcare for illegal aliens is an enormous addition to our entitlement programs cost in America. I would estimate the additional cost to taxpayers at a minimum of fifty billion dollars annually. Why should taxpayers be forced to fund criminal behavior in order for the Democrats to buy votes? It is shameful, illegal and a very transparent scheme."

"I agree completely," Willie replied. "Have you been involved with any open debate whatsoever on the issue of nationalized healthcare?" Joe smothered his urge to laugh.

"The Democrats are convinced they have the sixty

Senate votes to pass their healthcare boondoggle. They are

rubbing our noses in it by meeting behind closed doors and

then calling their decisions bipartisan. The American

people have no inkling what is going to happen when this

bill is rammed through Congress. The cost to taxpayers is

going to be enormous in terms of budget deficits, inflation

and drastic reduction in the quality of healthcare in the

United states. The bill contains over a thousand pages of

legal minutiae and will require a multi-billion dollar

bureaucracy to implement it. The cost figures are pure

guesswork and the savings are bogus as well. The actual

cost of every entitlement program in our history has been

grossly underestimated. To believe that nearly fifty million

people can be covered by the proposed healthcare

nationalization with resultant savings is nothing short of

moronic. The slashing of Medicare funding by half a

trillion dollars is not saving money. It is simply reducing

medical care for seniors in favor of a large segment of voters who have become dependent on government welfare and who will invariably vote for Democrats and their nanny government agenda. Senior citizens tend to vote for conservative Republicans. The Democrats intend to rob senior citizens to buy votes from those who pay no income tax."

Willie folded his hands across his notes. "I fail to see a single facet of nationalized healthcare that will benefit the American people. There will be less healthcare available at a much higher cost. There will be fewer citizens entering heath care professions because their earnings potential will be slashed to fund a cumbersome and unqualified government bureaucracy. There will be fewer hospitals and clinics and a long waiting list for diagnostic tests using advanced technology. Healthcare will be rationed and the elderly will be sacrificed for captured Democratic votes within the mushrooming welfare ranks. The Democrats are spouting

the same nonsense about nationalized healthcare as they

have about socialism being superior to capitalism. The

bind, deaf and dumb radical liberals think they will succeed

where everyone else has failed. There is not a single

country where socialized medicine has benefited its

citizens. In every instance where it has been experimented

with the results have been disastrous. People wait months

for diagnostic tests. In some countries doctors conduct

group office visits. There are fewer doctors trying to see

more patients as more professionals exit the practice of

medicine."

Joe nodded his agreement. "Numerous hospitals and

clinics will close due to shrinking revenues. More and

more taxpayer funding will be required to support

inadequate facilities. Socialism does not make healthcare

more efficient. It makes it both scarce and more expensive.

Socialized medicine is plagued by the same negative

factors as socialized manufacturing. Individual incentive is

eliminated by the system causing productivity to drop and

costs to rise. There has never been an exception to this

predictable pattern. Humans can never be stimulated to

higher levels of personal productivity by reducing their

benefits."

"The stimulus package is another loser but it is also

intended to buy votes," Willie added. "The five hundred to

a thousand dollar stimulus checks will have very little

impact on the overall economy. People tend to either save

the money for an emergency or spend it on entertainment.

Every nation that has tried to spend its way out of a

recession has failed miserably. The Japanese tried several

cycles of stimulus checks without any significant impact on

their economy. All they really accomplished was to add a

few hundred billion to their national debt. The Democrats

favor the stimulus package because it maintains the nanny

government image that produces votes from those paying

no income taxes."

Willie moved on to the issue of bailing out banks with

taxpayers money.

"What effect have you seen on our economy due to the

hundreds of billions of taxpayers dollars loaned to banks

for the purpose of maintaining a flow of credit to

American businesses?"

Joe snorted with contempt. "Heiny Takmore was more

focused on keeping his banker friends solvent and

protecting his own investments. With few exceptions, the

banks gobbled up the money to pay multi-million dollar

salaries and even more ridiculous bonuses. There was very

minimal impact on the creation of jobs through credit flow

for business expansion. I do believe the banks will repay

most of the bailout money but I predict the taxpayers will

lose roughly a hundred and fifty billion dollars in

nonpayment and interest losses."

"What I don't understand, Joe, is why the banks should

have it both ways. They make vulgar profits on risky

business decisions and then get bailed out when they make

risky decisions and lose their shirt. That is not how the free

market operates. The bailout benefited no one but the same

executives who bankrupted their organizations."

"That is true." Joe commented. "The Democrats

controlling Congress wanted a shot at taking over the

banking industry just like they want to nationalize

healthcare. They never really expected that the banks

would be able to repay the money soon enough to avoid a

government takeover as the major stockholder."

"We'll find out in a few months. Thank you, Senator.

We want you back real soon."

CHAPTER SIX

Election day triggered continuous coverage of the political scene by all the major TV networks. Shep Spitz and Kelly Smith hosted Telitright coverage. Shep looked sharp and well groomed as usual in his tailor made gray suit, pale blue shirt and red tie. He was quite handsome and very articulate. He glanced at the poll numbers being posted.

"Early results indicate a six point Democratic lead in the large urban areas in the northeast and a three point lead in Virginia, Florida and North Carolina. McPaign is running four points ahead in the South and Midwest. The polls are holding fairly steady. The vote count is just beginning in the western time zone. According to

Democrat supporting pollsters Phew, USA Yesterday,

Canter, WeeklyNews, CBC, ABN, and Trollup, the

Democrats are expected to take Washington, Oregon,

Nevada, California, Colorado and New Mexico in the west;

Minnesota, Iowa, Wisconsin, Illinois, Michigan, Indiana

and Ohio in the Midwest and northern states; and virtually

all the states along the eastern seaboard except South

Carolina and Georgia. Republicans are expected to prevail

in the other twenty-one states plus Alaska. Hawaii is

expected to go to the Democrats. If these projections

materialize, the Democrats will take control of both the

Congress and White House and appoint enough US

Supreme Court justices to ensure a liberal court for the next

three administrations. Rumors are surfacing that at least

three justices will time their retirements to allow a liberal

Democratic president to appoint their replacements." Shep

paused and scanned the big board.

"In addition, should these polls be accurate, it will mean that the large urban areas containing the most welfare recipients and the most families paying no income tax will elect the President and majority of Congressional seats up for reelection. There is little doubt that this voting pattern will continue. When ten million illegal aliens get the vote it will give the Democrats an ongoing voting majority and spell the end of our traditional American way of life. Socialism will replace capitalism and we will be steered toward world government. Let's hope and pray that the poll numbers are wrong and radical liberal Democrats do not take total control of our government. Of course there is always the possibility that the Democrats in their arrogance will do something outrageously stupid like nationalizing healthcare and allowing continued deflation of the U.S. dollar. When the government runs out of credit, who is going to feed the Democratic voting majority?"   Shep checked the board again but saw no change worthy of explanation.

"The rich who have been investing in America will invest where they get a reasonable return on risks taken. They can leave a disintegrating United States and enjoy lives of luxury elsewhere. Unemployment will escalate with the flight of American capitalists. Russia and Eastern Europe provide excellent investment opportunities as these nations convert from communism to capitalism." Shep turned toward Kelly. "Kelly has some breaking news from Iran."

Kelly looked stunning in her low cut red dress that set off her gorgeous figure, naturally blonde hair and beautiful face. "Iranian citizens protesting President Sohon Slobberingjon's oppressive administration and alleged election fraud are rioting in the streets of Tehran."

Live coverage of the chaos in Tehran flashed on the TV

screens. Demonstrators were being beaten back by

helmeted police and sprayed with tear gas and water

cannons. Signs and placards denounced Slobberingjon and

demanded his removal from office.

Kelly looked into her main camera and continued:

"The protestors are hoping for support from the United

States but America's response will be delayed until the

election here is determined. In other news, two alleged

Islamic terrorists have been apprehended by British

authorities trying to board a plane at Heathrow Airport in

London. The Boeing 747 with 268 passengers on board

was scheduled to land at JFK in New York at 10:47 this

morning. The two bearded Arabs in their early thirties were

identified as Abduhl Behedu and Muhammad Ali

Blowutomecca. The two were taken into custody when a

canine cop sniffed out their plastic explosives taped inside

their underwear."

Kelly wasn't quite able to smother laughter and Shep chuckled in deep amusement. "I don't know about you, Kelly, but I can't help wondering what those Jihad warriors were going to do with those seventy-two brown eyed virgins awaiting their sudden arrival in Paradise." Kelly blushed slightly. "Should have thought about that before donating such necessary appendages."

The presidential candidates mingled with avid supporters at their respective campaign headquarters watching the tail end of the election results being televised. Barry Osama was cool and confident. The ballot boxes in the swing states had been stuffed faithfully by Forenborn recruits and their half-witted accomplices. The threatened investigations by state authorities never materialized beyond the talking stage when it became apparent that the election fraud was not really a major factor in the election outcome.

Osama was going to get approximately nine million eight hundred thousand more votes than McPaign. The pundits declared Barry Osama the next president of the United States and McPaign gave his obligatory concession speech. The liberal news media, Georgie Sorrow and Americans on the government dole had foisted the man from Mombosa into the White House.

The inaugural ball was overly extravagant and attended by liberal media anchors with thrills running up their legs and heavy contributors to the Osama election campaign. Also invited were a couple dozen Hollywood celebrities who mingled with con artists, tax cheats, socialists, communists, abortionists, homosexuals, and domestic terrorists. Most of the liberal Democratic members of Congress and two Supreme Court justices filtered through the merrymakers.

It was Osama's big night and he exhibited a strange

mixture of arrogance and charm. The dining, drinking and

dancing continued through the Cinderella hour. Shortly

after midnight Barry and Jemama cordially thanked the

attendees and headed for their hotel room. The exit of the

Osama's dampened the partying spirit and the crowd began

breaking up and drifting into the cool morning air.

Glen Ripuone appeared somewhat melancholy sitting

across from Jim McPaign and Sarah Planke. The United

States had its first African born black Muslim president and

the losing candidates had agreed to appear on Glen's talk

show to review the future administration's campaign

promises.

"I know it has been a long and hard fought campaign,"

Glen ventured. "On behalf of Telitright News, I want to

express sincere appreciation for both of you appearing here

this morning. Were either of you surprised that Osama

carried twenty-eight states, 365 electoral votes and roughly

53.7 of the popular vote?"

Jim looked somber but well rested. "Not really. We

knew he would carry ninety to ninety-five percent of the

Afro-American votes. He had over forty-five percent of the

popular vote in his pocket from the beginning of the

campaign. Of course, we're speaking of the citizens on

welfare, the majority of which don't want a job, and those

who are employed but pay no income taxes. They believed

whatever the far left media elected to broadcast and

swallowed Osama's velvet rhetoric about an expansion of

entitlement programs and more government subsidies to

feed and house them."

"The main street media gave Osama a free pass," Sarah

added. "Moreover, their radically liberal anchors labeled

anyone a redneck racist who dared question his birthplace

and lack of experience or his choice of personal mentors,

friends and associates. When Osama admitted in his book

that he was mentored by a hard core communist, the

anchors at WeeklyNews never said anything. When he also

wrote in another of his books, 'I stand with the Muslims

should the political winds shift in an ugly direction,' the

liberal media said nothing. When he admitted in his books

that he chose Marxist friends and professors in college, the

liberal network anchors and newspapers ignored his

admissions. When he traveled to Pakistan using a non-U.S.

passport and swore himself to be a foreign student to get

financial aid in California, the media ignored his admission

he was foreign born. When his paternal grandmother,

Mombosa hospital officials, local ministers and Kenyan

ambassador to the United States stated he was born in

Mombosa, Kenya, the liberal TV networks and newspapers

reported rednecks and racists were fabricating lies about

Osama being foreign born." Jim felt compelled to add to

what Sarah had pointed out concerning the liberal media.

"When he admitted his spiritual father was a rabid

racist who railed against the United States, the liberal

pundits said it didn't matter. When the Palestinians raised

money for his election campaign, their motive was never

questioned by the liberal media. When he was endorsed by

Louis Farrakhan, Mummar Kadaffi and Hugo Chavez, the

liberal media said it didn't count for much. When

Teleitright News pointed out that he had no experience of

any kind other than as mouthpiece for a racially oriented

activist organization called Forenborn, the liberal media

said it didn't matter. When he refused to wear the American

flag pin and placed his hand over his groin for the playing

of our national anthem, the liberal media gave him another

pass." Sarah threw a few more logs on the funeral pyre:

"When Osama said he believed humans evolved from lower life forms and favored homosexual orientation beginning at the kindergarten level, the liberal media fawned over his brilliance and got thrills up their legs. When he surrounded himself with communists, socialists, domestic terrorists, racial agitators, and ex-convicts, the liberal media praised him for his wisdom in selecting personal advisers and consultants. Telitright News was the only TV network that made any effort whatsoever to report the news rather than to invent the news. However, very few of those who voted for Osama watch Telitright News."

Jim followed up with additional comments. "The only voters who had a clue to Osama's unsavory background and foreign birth were Conservatives and Republicans plus a few moderate Democrats. When the black vote went ninety-five percent for Osama and the liberal media swooned over his candidacy, he pulled in an extra 3.7 of the popular vote. The number of states he carried and the

total electoral votes allocated to him are less than academic

because of the all or nothing rule in most states pertaining

to electoral tallying which determines the number of states

colored blue. Actually, with a rubber stamp media and near

majority of voters depending upon government handouts,

Osama's margin of victory being less than four percent of

the popular vote is not exactly a ringing endorsement. He

rode public ignorance and Christian apathy into the White

House. The far left wing media blindly loyal to the liberal

democrats brainwashed a willingly ignorant American

public into electing the black knight from Mombosa who is

pro-Palestinian, pro-Muslim extremist, anti-American,

communist oriented, pro-abortion, a homosexual activist,

and totally dedicated to helping Georgie Sorrow and like

minded radical liberals steer the United States into being

absorbed by a global government system controlled by a

socialist dictator."

Glen had been mute while Jim and Sarah responded to his initial question. He was totally dismayed.

"I prepared a summary of Osama's major campaign promises intended to influence the ninety and one half million people who voted that never attended college and therefore have an uneducated perception of free market economics, foreign policy, and devaluation of our dollar. Osama promised these voters a redistribution of our national wealth by cutting taxes on the working class and raising taxes on those with incomes over $250,000. He promised a revamped national healthcare system which covers all Americans while saving billions of dollars. He promised a change in foreign policy that is premised upon unconditional negotiations with terrorists and rogue states like Iran and North Korea, plus reductions in military expenditures. He promised to bring peace to the Middle

East by putting pressure on Israel to make concessions to

Palestinians. He promised to create millions of new jobs

including an emphasis on clean energy innovations. He

promised an excess profit tax on major oil and gasoline

producers. He promised to lower carbon dioxide emissions

by taxing those businesses that use coal for energy

production and by more demanding standards on motor

vehicle emissions. He promised hundreds of millions in

taxpayer dollars to develop clean energy sources. He

promised the unions his full support and his adoption of

union objectives. He promised to bring the wars in Iraq and

Afghanistan to a successful conclusion within two years

and bring the troops home. He promised American citizen

civil rights and lawyers to terrorists being detained by the

United States. He promised to solve the problems

connected with illegal aliens. He promised a better

standard of living for the working class and those on

welfare and other government assistance by lowering the standard of living enjoyed by the rich capitalist fat cats and wall street investors."

Glen looked from Jim to Sarah. "Since the liberal media never questioned his ability to deliver on campaign promises, it is understandable why the working class and those being suckled by the government hailed him as "the Chosen One" and as their Messiah. Can either of you see any possibility that Osama can deliver on these promises without transforming America into a radical socialist nation?"

Both Jim and Sarah gave Glen a negative wag of their heads. Jim took the lead. "We currently have the most corrupt and deceitful administration in the history of the United States. Even worse, they now have a death grip on our federal government. The U.S. Constitution might as well be hung as toilet paper in the Congressional bathrooms. Each Democratic administration since Harry

Truman has reinterpreted and rewritten our Constitution to

accommodate their creeping socialist agendas. They have

now finally realized their goal of a radically liberal

Congress and White House plus a super majority in both

the House and Senate. Thus, they can ram though whatever

laws they deem fit without even consulting the Republican

minority. The U.S. Supreme Court is evenly split between

liberals and conservatives with the swing vote favoring the

liberals." Jim voiced his major concern:

"Truthfully, Glen, unless the Congressional balance of

power changes in the 2010 mid-term elections, there is no

legal way to stop the radical transformation of this country

into a socialist nation. Osama cannot possibly deliver on

his campaign promises because the United States does not

exist in a vacuum. Our economy is now inexorably linked

to the economies of other nations as demonstrated by the

financial panic around the world when several major U.S.

banks became insolvent. Attempts by the Osama admini-

stration to implement his political objectives will result in

massive devaluation of the U.S. dollar. When that happens,

the U.S. will be unable to borrow enough money in the

world credit markets to stay solvent as a nation. Our

absolute bankruptcy may be delayed as our primary

creditors try to prop us up with loans so we can keep

consuming their goods and services which drives their own

economies. Nevertheless, at some point in the near future,

running our money presses around the clock will reduce

the value of the dollar to the point where our creditors will

cut their losses and dump us entirely. Then we will witness

the fall of the United States into the cesspool of global

government. The transition will be accompanied by mass

starvation and total anarchy. Historically, anarchy has

never been quelled without a ruthless dictator rising to

absolute power. The anarchy in the United States will

quickly spread around the globe."

Glen leaned back, closed his eyes momentarily and then

looked from Jim to Sarah. "The seeds of the imminent

global financial collapse was planted nearly a century ago.

The two principal Rothschild representatives in New York,

J. P. Morgan Co., and Kuhn, Loeb & Co. were the firms

which set up the Jekyll Island Conference at which the

Federal Reserve Act was drafted making possible the

subsequent successful and sneaky campaign to have the

plan enacted into law by Congress, and the same

Rothschild agents purchased the controlling amount of

stock in the Federal Reserve Bank of New York in 1914.

These same banking conglomerates had their principal

officers appointed to the Federal Reserve Board of

Governors and the Federal Advisory Council in 1914.

Then, conspiring individuals owning controlling stock in

existing banks caused those banks to purchase controlling

shares in the Federal Reserve regional banks. So this was a

master plan by the Rothschild family to own the U.S.

monetary supply through the Federal Reserve and having

their co-conspirators control the flow of capital. The list of

conspirators included JP Morgan, Brown Bros, Harriman,

Lazard Bros NY, Drexel & Company, Schroder Bank,

Solomon Loeb and The Lehman Brothers, who jointly

formed the Federal Reserve Bank Of New York. The

major shareholders were National City Bank N.Y. now

Citibank. The major shareholders of National City Bank

N.Y were Rockefeller, JP Morgan, Payne family, Stilliman

family, and the Edison family (now GE Company). This

alliance of banking conglomerates control the Federal

Reserve and consequently the issuance of federally

secured loans in the U.S. The Rockefeller family,

Goldman Sachs, Lehman Brothers, Rothschild Family,

Warburg Family, the IMF (international arm) and JP

Morgan Chase control the federal reserve system for

without them, the Federal Reserve System could not

function."

The expression on Sarah's face indicated she knew

nothing of the private control of the Federal Reserve

System. Jim was somewhat knowledgeable of the private

manipulation of the U.S. Treasury. He listened passively to

Glen's explanation as to how the U.S. dollar is knowingly

deflated:

"The power of those controlling the Federal Reserve in

1914 was limited because every dollar was convertible to

an established amount of Gold which was difficult to

manipulate since each nation controlled its own supply of

gold bullion. This changed drastically in July, 1944 when

the U.S. and 44 Allied nations met at Bretton Woods,

New Hampshire for the United Nations Monetary and

Financial Conference. The delegates hammered out and

signed the Bretton Woods Agreements setting up a system

including rules, procedures and bureaucracies to control

and regulate the international monetary system. This

agreement gave birth to the World Bank and the IMF as

we know it today. The Bretton Woods economic system

required fixed exchange rates indexed to an existing

money supply dubbed 'the reserve currency.' This placed a

lot of trust in the Federal Reserve System which was

selected as stewards of this reserve currency. This new

economic system was backed up by the Gold Standard

allowing imbalances in international trade to be rectified

automatically. A country with a deficit national debt would

have depleted gold reserves and would thus have to reduce

its money supply. The resulting fall in domestic demand for

goods would reduce imports and the lowering of prices

would boost exports thereby rectifying the deficit. The

strength of the U.S. economy and the fixed relationship of

the dollar to gold plus the commitment of the U.S. govern-

ment to convert dollars into gold made the dollar the best

choice for the reserve currency."

Sarah began to see where Glen was headed.

"Economic instability during the Nixon administration

forced the U.S. to eliminate the fixed gold price which

caused the gold standard system to break down. This meant

that a fixed amount of dollars would no longer be worth

one ounce of gold and that all fixed currencies against the

dollar were effectively under the control of the Federal

Reserve and its shareholders."

"Exactly," Glen replied. "The U.S. Dollar became

what is known as a 'fiat currency' based on nothing but

U.S. borrowing power thereby allowing the Federal

Reserve to freely manipulate the money supply. This gold

standard breakdown and the unwanted control of other

currencies by the Federal Reserve System resulted in the

introduction of the Euro in January 1999.   In order for the

Rothschilds to regain their manipulating position they

needed a one world currency and a one world government.

To usher in a global currency and world government, the

U.S. dollar must be destroyed and that is precisely what the

Osama administration is committed to accomplishing by

bankrupting the United States. That is why Osama has

surrounded himself with socialists, communists, con artists

and black demagogues to convince a voting majority that

they are oppressed and exploited by capitalism."

Both Jim and Sarah were now beginning to understand

why Georgie Sorrow spent a billion dollars to get Osama

into the White House backed by a majority in both houses

of Congress along with two ultra liberal Supreme Court

Justices. Georgie wants a global currency and one world

government.

Glen now ripped the final cover off the strategy to bankrupt America. "The banking conglomerates created exotic derivatives and options based upon real estate mortgages secured by non-existent collateral to create more money out of thin air from the money that was made out of thin air through the Federal Reserve while at the same time hiding the housing bubble from regulators through the mind numbing complexity of the derivatives and banking deregulation. Therefore, this fiat currency system is set up to fail and devalue the U.S. dollar to the point of national bankruptcy. The fiat currency system works to keep everyone involved in debt forever with the banking conglomerates raking in enormous profits. Thus, when the banking conglomerates go belly up, so does the U.S. Treasury. For example, the Federal Reserve loans a private investment bank 500 million at 3 % permitting the bank to loan out 5 billion at 4 and a quarter percent to retail banks and other financial institutions which in turn loan out

the 5 billion at five and three quarters % primarily as real

estate mortgages secured by exotic mortgage derivatives

worth only 50% of the outstanding loans. If 25% of the

loans default, the retail banks and other financial

institutions have lost roughly one and a quarter billion

dollars plus 4 and a quarter % interest. Thus, if U.S.

investment banks over a period of ten years have borrowed

6 trillion from the Federal Reserve and the mortgage

default rate rises to 25%, the retail banks and financial

institutions stand to lose 10 to 15 trillion plus the

contractual interest rate. The investment banks along with

the retail banks and financial institutions go belly up and

the resulting Federal Reserve loss adds a few trillion to the

U.S. national debt. Then, the Osama administration adds a

few more trillion in entitlement programs and the value of

the dollar falls like a heavy rock."

Sarah now saw the big picture. "So, now the problem becomes how to pay back the Fed while the economy is in shambles, and the only way to do that is to borrow even more money from the Federal Reserve at 3%. Because the Fed manipulated by the banking conglomerates controls the money supply, the fiat currency system is intentionally designed to keep everyone in debt forever. The money can never be paid back and the national debt must get bigger and bigger to keep the economy from collapsing. This is why capitalistic societies have advanced way beyond countries that don't utilize interest such as most Muslim countries. The fiat currency system has directly benefited the stockholders of the banking conglomerates which control the Federal Reserve and allowed them to amass vulgar wealth and immense power." Sarah sighed with disgust and Glen painted the bankruptcy picture:

"Bankruptcy is inevitable when there is no more

capacity or means to repay the Federal Reserve.   And this

scenario has been escalating over the course of the Hush

administration, which has been raped of its entire

manufacturing base by massive off shoring of jobs to

China and India by multinational corporations in order to

remain competitive in world markets. The U.S. citizens can

not pay any of this money back because the U.S. has been

sterilized by excessive labor cost from manufacturing

goods and services that people want and are willing to

import. When jobs are exported, U.S. citizens cannot pay

back the retail banks which in turn cannot pay back the

investment banks which in turn cannot pay back the

Federal Reserve and the federal treasury is insufficient to

pay back the creditor nations who loaned the U.S. the

money by buying U.S. bonds to keep the money presses

rolling further deflating the U.S. dollar."

Glen pushed the button his desk and the video screen

descended into viewing position. "Osama and Sorrow are

utilizing the Cloward-Piven strategy for bankrupting the

United States. This video is an excellent presentation of

the strategy preached by two communist professors who

hate America. I will set up a slow scroll and we can read it

together."

The screen lit up and the lettering scrolled upward at

normal reading speed:

"Strategy for forcing political change through orchestrated

crisis"

First proposed in 1966 and named after Columbia

University sociologists Richard Andrew Cloward and his

wife Frances Fox Piven (today Piven is an honorary chair

for the Democratic Socialists of America), the "Cloward-

Piven Strategy" seeks to hasten the fall of capitalism by

overloading the government bureaucracy with a flood of impossible demands, thus pushing society into crisis and economic collapse.

Inspired by the August 1965 riots in the black district of Watts in Los Angeles, Cloward and Piven published an article titled "The Weight of the Poor: A Strategy to End Poverty" in a popular socialist magazine. Following its publication, the magazine sold an unprecedented 30,000 reprints. Activists were abuzz over the so-called "crisis strategy" or "Cloward-Piven Strategy," as it came to be called. Many were eager to put it into effect.

In their 1966 article, Cloward and Piven charged that the ruling classes used welfare to weaken the poor; that by providing a social safety net, the rich doused the fires of rebellion. Poor people can advance only when "the rest of society is afraid of them," Cloward told ardent supporters on September 27, 1970.

Rather than placating the poor with government hand-

outs, wrote Cloward and Piven, activists should work to

sabotage and destroy the welfare system; the collapse of

the welfare state would ignite a political and financial crisis

that would rock the nation; poor people would rise in

revolt; only then would "the rest of society" accept their

demands.

The key to sparking this rebellion would be to expose

the inadequacy of the welfare state. Cloward-Piven's early

promoters cited radical organizer Saul Alinsky as their

inspiration. "Make the enemy live up to their own book of

rules," Alinsky wrote in his 1972 book . When pressed to

honor every word of every law and statute, every Judaeo-

Christian moral tenet, and every implicit promise of the

liberal social contract, human agencies inevitably fall short.

The system's failure to "live up" to its rule book can then

be used to discredit it altogether, and to replace the

capitalist "rule book" with a socialist one.

The authors noted that the number of Americans subsisting on welfare -- about 8 million, at the time -- probably represented less than half the number who were technically eligible for full benefits. They proposed a "massive drive to recruit the poor the welfare rolls." Cloward and Piven calculated that persuading even a fraction of potential welfare recipients to demand their entitlements would bankrupt the system.

The result, they predicted, would be "a profound financial and political crisis" that would unleash "powerful forces ... for major economic reform at the national level."

Their article called for "cadres of aggressive organizers" to use "demonstrations to create a climate of militancy." Intimidated by threats of black violence, politicians would appeal to the federal government for help. Carefully orchestrated media campaigns, carried out

by friendly, left wing journalists, would float the idea of "a
federal program of income redistribution," in the form of a
guaranteed living income for all -- working and non-
working people alike.

Local officials would clutch at this idea like
drowning men to a lifeline. They would apply pressure on
Washington to implement it. With every major city
erupting into chaos, Washington would have to act.

This was an example of what are commonly called
Trojan Horse movements -- mass movements whose
outward purpose seems to be providing material help to the
downtrodden, but whose real objective is to draft poor
people into service as revolutionary foot soldiers; to
mobilize poor people to overwhelm government agencies
with a flood of demands beyond the capacity of those
agencies to meet.

The flood of demands was calculated to break the

budget, jam the bureaucratic gears into gridlock, and bring

the system crashing down. Fear, turmoil, violence and

economic collapse would accompany such a breakdown --

providing perfect conditions for fostering radical change.

That was the theory.

Cloward and Piven recruited a militant black organizer

named George Wiley to lead their new movement. In the

summer of 1967, Wiley founded the National Welfare

Rights Organization (NWRO). His tactics closely followed

the recommendations set out in Cloward and Piven's

article. His followers invaded welfare offices across the

United States -- often violently -- bullying social workers

and loudly demanding every penny to which the law

"entitled" them.

By 1969, NWRO claimed a dues-paying membership

of 22,500 families, with 523 chapters across the nation.

Acting out Wiley's tactics, there were sit-ins in

legislative chambers, including a United States Senate committee hearing, mass demonstrations of several thousand welfare recipients, school boycotts, picket lines, mounted police, tear gas, arrests - and, on occasion, rock-throwing, smashed glass doors, overturned desks, scattered papers and ripped-out phones. These methods proved effective. The violence and overloading strategy succeeded beyond Wiley's wildest dreams.

From 1965 to 1974, the number of households on welfare soared from 4.3 million to 10.8 million, despite mostly flush economic times. By the early 1970s, one person was on the welfare rolls in New York City for every two working in the city's private economy. As a direct result of its massive welfare spending, New York City was forced to declare bankruptcy in 1975. The entire state of New York nearly went down with it.

The Cloward-Piven strategy had proved its quick

effectiveness.

The Cloward-Piven strategy depended on surprise. Once society recovered from the initial shock, the backlash began. New York's welfare crisis horrified America, giving rise to a reform movement which culminated in "the end of welfare as we know it" -- the 1996 Personal Responsibility and Work Opportunity Reconciliation Act, which imposed time limits on federal welfare, along with strict eligibility and work requirements. Both Cloward and Piven attended the White House signing of the bill as guests of President Clinton.

Most Americans to this day have never heard of Cloward and Piven. But New York City Mayor Rudolph Giuliani attempted to expose them in the late 1990s. As his drive for welfare reform gained momentum, Giuliani accused the militant scholars by name, citing their 1966 manifesto as evidence that they had engaged in deliberate economic sabotage.

"This wasn't an accident," Giuliani charged in a July 20, 1998 speech. "It wasn't an atmospheric thing, it wasn't supernatural. This is the result of policies and programs designed to have the maximum number of people get on welfare."

Cloward and Piven never again revealed their intentions as candidly as they had in their 1966 article. Even so, their activism in subsequent years continued to rely on the tactic of overloading the system. When the public caught on to their welfare scheme, Cloward and Piven simply moved on, applying pressure to other sectors of the bureaucracy, wherever they detected weakness.In 1982, partisans of the Cloward-Piven strategy founded a new "voting rights movement," which purported to take up the unfinished work of the Voting Rights Act of 1965. Like ACORN, the organization that spear-headed this campaign, the new "voting rights" movement was led by veterans of

George Wiley's welfare rights crusade. Its flagship

organizations were Project Vote and Human SERVE, both

founded in 1982. Project Vote is an ACORN front group,

launched by former NWRO organizer and ACORN co-

founder Zach Polett. Human SERVE was founded by

Richard A. Cloward and Frances Fox Piven, along with a

former NWRO organizer named Hulbert James.

All three of these organizations -- ACORN, Project

Vote and Human SERVE -- set to work lobbying

energetically for the so-called Motor-Voter law, which Bill

Clinton ultimately signed in 1993. The Motor-Voter bill is

largely responsible for swamping the voter rolls with "dead

wood" -- invalid registrations signed in the name of

deceased, ineligible or non-existent people - thus opening

the door to the unprecedented levels of voter fraud and

"voter disenfranchisement" claims that followed in

subsequent elections.

At the White House signing ceremony for the Motor-Voter bill, both Richard Cloward and Frances Fox Piven were in attendance.

The new "voting rights" coalition combines mass voter registration drives - typically featuring high levels of fraud - with systematic intimidation of election officials in the form of frivolous lawsuits, unfounded charges of "racism" and "disenfranchisement," and "direct action" (street protests, violent or otherwise). Just as they swamped America's welfare offices in the 1960s, Cloward-Piven devotees now seek to overwhelm the nation's understaffed and poorly policed electoral system.

Their tactics set the stage for the Florida recount crisis of 2000, and have introduced a level of fear, tension and foreboding to U.S. elections previously encountered mainly in Third World countries.

In January 2010, journalist John Fund reported that

Congressman Barney Frank and U.S. Senator Chuck

Schumer were preparing to unveil legislation calling for

"universal voter registration," whereby any person whose

name was on any federal roll at all -- be it a list of welfare

recipients, food stamp recipients, unemployment

compensation recipients, licensed drivers, convicted felons,

property owners, etc.--would automatically be registered to

vote in political elections. Without corresponding identity-

verification measures at polling places, such a law would

vastly expand the pool of eligible voters, thereby multiply-

ing the opportunities for fraudulent voters to cast ballots

under other people's names.

Both the Living Wage and Voting Rights movements

depend heavily on financial support from George Soros's

Open Society Institute and his "Shadow Party," through

whose support the Cloward-Piven strategy continues to

provide a blueprint for some of the Left's most ambitious

campaigns to overload, and cause the collapse of, various

American institutions.

Leftists such as Barack Obama euphemistically refer

to this collapse as a "fundamental transformation ," on the

theory that society can only be improved by destroying the

deeply flawed existing order and replacing it with what

they view as a better alternative...............

Glen shut down the projector and raised the viewing

screen back into idle position. He turned back to face Jim

and Sarah:

"To you and I who are modestly educated, those two

summaries were fairly straightforward and reasonably

understandable with an average level of concentration.

However approximately thirty percent of Americans do not

possess an adequate vocabulary to even read the statements; and another twenty percent might muddle through the narratives but not have a clue as to what is being outlined. Therein lies the opportunity for a political demagogue and oily manipulator like Barry Osama to lead the willingly ignorant to lower levels of poverty like a lead goat leading a flock of sheep to the slaughter. Osama takes away their freedom while promising them a utopia which he can never deliver. In the process his supporters among the masses are worse off and he makes strides toward his ultimate goal of absolute power to control every aspect of their lives."

Jim hung his head and breathed deeply. Sarah wiped tears from the corners of her eyes. Jim looked up at Glen. "I don't know how to make people swooning over Osama understand because they really don't want to hear what a fraud he really is. They want to believe the lies he is feeding them and have closed their minds to the fact that he might be a communist like his father, and he wants to rule

over them and let them share equal poverty while he lives

like an Arab king."

Sarah put her handkerchief back into her suit pocket and

spoke with a tone of deep sadness:

"You can predict exactly what Osama's game plan is by

reading Alinsky's Rules for Radicals. Osama taught those

rules to Forenborn's recruits and he follows the rules

himself without deviation. Alinsky had a keen understand-

ing of human nature and knew exactly how to exploit

willing ignorance to achieve very devious political

objectives."

Glen thought about Sarah's comments and decided he

had nothing more to add. "Where do you two go from

here? Any particular political strategy?"

Jim smiled at the question. "I'll go back and work in

the Senate to try and slow down Osama's bankrupt America

agenda. I'll also work to build the Republican party and

hope for a change in the Congressional balance of power in

2010. In his arrogance and egomania, Osama may lose his

majority."

"How about you, Sarah?" Glen asked. "Will you

continue to challenge corruption in Washington?" "Only

as Governor of my state, Glen. Based on the 2008 election

results, I believe I can best serve my country in my role as

Governor for the next several months. After that, I will

reevaluate my options."

CHAPTER SEVEN

Bill Smiley did a monologue before welcoming his guests. He relaxed in his studio setting and smiled into the cameras.

"President Osama and First Lady Jemama went on a date for married couples with children Saturday night. Barry spent a cool million of the taxpayers' dollars taking Jemama out for dinner. Barry wants the taxpayers to "tighten their belts" and sacrifice for the greater good of America but sees no hypocrisy in blowing a million dollars of the taxpayers' money simply showing Jemama a good time and dining out in New York. Since Barry and Jemama already live in a mansion surrounded by a host of servants and personal attendants which already cost the taxpayers a couple million bucks; and since the White House has every

convenience imaginable, why would Barry feel justified in

flying with Jemama to New York just to take in a show and

eat a bite? They could have dined at home in lavish style

with their own chef and personal attendants without

shutting down busy New York streets and the ferry to New

Jersey for two hours. The little bite to eat and show in New

York required three planes to transport Barry, Jemama,

aides and reporters from Washington to New York, plus

two helicopters to ferry Barry, Jemama and their party to

and from the airports. Then add to those expenses limo

service, Secret Service agents, military guard and fuel for

the multiple planes and helicopters. Moreover, thousands

of taxpayers wearing very tight belts were inconvenienced

to the point their whole evening was spoiled. Such

extravagance is the arrogant, self-centered, mindset of the

African born, Muslim communist demagogue occupying

our White House. Osama is not alone in his blatant

hypocrisy. The Congressional thieves bankrupting our great

nation locked in their Cadillac health insurance plan plus

hikes in salary and benefits while denying those living on

Social Security a cost of living increase. Just to show their

absolute contempt for hard working, tax paying Americans

the gluttonous hogs also raised taxes through increased

healthcare premiums coupled with reductions in healthcare

benefits for senior citizens. However, for those not paying

taxes and living on government handouts, the fat cat

members of Congress increased their benefits and will pay

their healthcare insurance costs. Of course, these same free

loading citizens can be relied upon to keep voting

Democratic. To really demonstrate their undying devotion

to our nation, numerous members of the Congress and the

Osama administration cheat on their tax returns. Most

American citizens seem to agree that most politicians in

Washington today are feathering their own nests rather than serving the people. Perhaps it's time to gas up the pig trucks. The typical liberal Democrats' excuses for failure to deliver on any of their utopian promises after they have taken over total control of our government are mirrored by excuses given for Osama's failure to bring the 2016 Olympic games to Chicago."

Bill grinned with easy humor. "First and foremost it is Walter Hush's fault. Second, the International Olympic Committee is racist. Third, there were not a sufficient number of wise Latino judges on the committee. Fourth, Osama's trip was not about bringing the games to Chicago, it was about the number of Olympic games "saved" or "created." Fifth, we've been quite clear all along that we did not want the Olympics in Chicago. Sixth, it must be obvious that no president could have pulled this off. Seventh, the real problem was Israel building settlements in land taken during the Arab-Israeli wars. Eighth, who

cares if Osama couldn't talk the committee into Chicago

hosted Olympic games; he will convince Iran to abandon

their nuclear weapons program. Ninth, Osama was

distracted by a brief meeting with General Stoopenbow.

Tenth, dead people can't vote on the committee like they do

in Chicago."

Bill had to chuckle at excuse number ten. "We'll

squeeze in an early commercial and be right back to

welcome our esteemed guests: White House Chief of Staff,

Colin Coldfish; Treasury Secretary, Timmy Notax; and

General Leon Stoopenbow."

Somenie Bucs sipped tea in his private office with his

Internal Audit Deputy, Choosu Yens. From his seventh

story office window he glanced nervously at the traffic

flowing steadily along the streets in downtown Peking. The

diamond rings on both his hands flashed in the afternoon sunlight as he rubbed both temples to ease a persistent headache.

He was sixty-nine, plump and bald. His typical oriental features were leathery and deeply wrinkled. His wobbly stomach tumbled over his belt as he belched from a heavy lunch.

Choosu was short, wiry, and petite with dark yellow skin and pencil mustache. He felt much sympathy for Somenie but an executive decision was long overdue. "Set bottom dollar value. Warn U.S.   Hit bottom.....change dollars for Euros."

Somenie breathed out a long despondent sigh. "Seven hundred fifty million vanish. Veri, veri bad. Lose soft job. Work data. We change lose fifty."

When the commercial faded, all three of Bill's guests

were seated and ready for some heavy grilling. General
Leon Stoopenbow appeared slim and athletic in his
General's uniform cluttered with a dozen or so medals. He
was sixty-three and cleanly barbered. His piercing blue
eyes, hawk nose and thin lips displayed no tension. Colin
Coldfish was a short tightly packed Jew with black curly
hair, amber eyes, shiny nose and arrogant personality.
Timmy Notax was sharply dressed thanks to cheating on
his taxes and gave the impression of a very important
business executive.

Bill had welcomed them to his talk show during the
commercial break. He addressed his first question to
General Stoopenbow. "General, we have been fighting
terrorists in Afghanistan since October 7, 2001. American
forces could have taken the entire Afghan land mass in less
than six months. Why are we still there?"

General Stoopenbow was not surprised by the opening

query.   "Because we are not fighting a war. We have

another Vietnam. You cannot tell the enemy from the

Afghan civilians. We are more concerned about civilian

deaths than we are about defeating the terrorists. As with

South Vietnam, we are supporting a weak local govern-

ment's efforts to maintain control of a highly volatile

situation. We are spending hundreds of billions in both

Afghanistan and Iraq to support their governments' military

and police forces while considering ourselves guests in

both terrorist infested countries. This guest banker

approach will never defeat the enemy because they are too

well armed, well funded, adequately supplied, well

organized and committed to fight to the death. They also

have a steady supply of volunteers willing to take on

suicide missions. We could not win in Vietnam for the

exact same reason."   The general's eyes narrowed.

"The Johnson and Nixon administrations would not

allow our military to win the war because of concerns over

civilian casualties and sensitive relations with other

countries including both allies and countries supplying us

with vital resources. We were fighting a guerrilla war on

their home turf with both hands tied behind our backs. The

politicians were more than willing to sacrifice nearly sixty

thousand of our troops and another hundred thousand

wounded to maintain their political power base. We are

doing precisely the same thing in both Afghanistan and

Iraq. It is absolute insanity. The rest of the world thinks we

are weak kneed, fickle, military morons and easy to

manipulate. Why should the North Koreans and the

Iranians fear us when we have blundered around in

Afghanistan for more than eight years and spent almost

seven years doing the same thing is Iraq. Our military

demonstrated very clearly during the first war with Iraq

how to win a war. We took the entire country in a matter of

weeks. The Iraqis had modern weapons, an eight hundred

thousand man standing army, a modern air force, armored

divisions, heavy artillery, tanks, and missiles plus billions

of dollars in cash." The general's tone became more

adamant.

"Our president did not try to direct the war from the

White House. He gave our military a free hand to do

whatever was necessary to win the war with non-nuclear

weapons. It was only after the war was won that the

administration in Washington started making military

decisions and decided to allow the enemy to regroup and

rearm. Wars are won by Generals and lost by politicians

listening to anti-war demonstrations and worrying about

losing some votes."

Bill studied General Stoopenbow pensively. The man

had guts. He had just put his career in serious jeopardy. "I

couldn't agree more, General. What should we do in your

opinion?"

The general did not hesitate. "We should attack in full force, kill the terrorists and avoid civilian casualties as much as possible without sacrificing military objectives. If the local government doesn't support the effort, put them in chains and supervise an election so the people can vote in new leadership. Then get out of the country and let the newly elected government take over completely. Then make it very clear to the world that we will do the same thing in any country which harbors terrorists attacking the United States."

Bill considered the general's answer and asked a follow-up question: "How long do you anticipate we can maintain this guest banker strategy attempting to merely hold the line against more devastating terrorist attacks?"

"Until the liberal radicals in Congress finish bankrupting the United States or until the American people are fed up with their sons and daughters dying on foreign soil without accomplishing anything. Of course, there is a third possibility. Our halfhearted military efforts may embolden the terrorists to launch another 9/11 magnitude attack on the United States and trigger an unrestrained reaction by our military which the jackasses in Washington would not dare to oppose for fear of being physically jerked out of office by an enraged American public."

"The end of apathy can be frightening and deadly," Bill responded. "I believe the terrorists know this is a possible reaction from American citizens and do not want to run such a risk. They will continue to carry out limited murder and mayhem until we get totally disenchanted with the war effort and simply pull out. Our present reluctance to inflict civilian casualties or to offend the Arab world encourages them to hide in Mosques and behind women and children from whence they can venture out occasionally and attack us and our allies. We need to become totally committed and less predictable."

"Absolutely, Bill. The first priority must be to modify our foreign policy. Our main concern as to offending the Arab world is maintaining our supply of foreign oil plus the fact that our president is a Muslim who has publicly stated that he stands with the Muslim world. With respect to non-Muslim nations, our main concerns are stability of the dollar and ability to enforce economic sanctions against rogue nations seeking to develop nuclear and biological weapons systems. We must decide whether we want to put up with terrorist attacks and very fickle and unpredictable allies or to dedicating all our resources and military power to serving the best interests of our own people. The driving motive behind our existing foreign policy is entirely economic and benefits less that ten percent of our population."

"General, why not simply close our borders and supply American people with American goods and services. We then advise the world that the government of the United States of America is committed only to serving and protecting Americans and preventing the spread of nuclear and biological weapons. We stop consuming the goods and services produced by foreign economies and thus control the value of our currency. By serving our own people we will be competing only against ourselves and do not have to be concerned with cheap labor in other countries or the rise and fall of currency markets. We have the agricultural capability to feed ourselves quite well. We have the manufacturing and technical resources to provide every American with a superior standard of living including every conceivable convenience. We have the most advanced technology on the planet if we stop exporting it."

"You're absolutely right. Bill. There is actually nothing

we need from other nations if we exploit our own

resources. We have enough petroleum reserves to supply

ourselves another forty years even if we do not discover

additional reserves. Forty years is more than adequate time

to develop alternative energy sources and the supporting

infrastructure. We have the military capability and the

technology to build an impregnable missile defense shield

around the United States and to deploy laser beam and

particle beam defenses in space along with nuclear

weapons systems. We can provide full employment for

Americans building these defenses and supplying all our

domestic goods and services. There is no reason

whatsoever that the United States cannot be a world unto

ourselves and pursue life, liberty, and the pursuit of

happiness. We are a mighty nation with 300 million

citizens. That is more than the population of the entire

world when North America was discovered at which time

the continent was a world unto itself and needed nothing

whatsoever from foreign countries. It could easily become

so again."

Bill was a little skeptical. "The two major problems I

see with that approach are existing foreign investments by

Americans and the U.S. Government plus U.S. military

bases, equipment, troops and civilians around the globe."

General Stoopenbow replied with a measured and

thoughtful tone. "We simply bring our weapons,

equipment, supplies and people back home to produce and

contribute within our own economy. Let the foreign hosts

take over the land mass we occupy now. We have enough

firepower to destroy the planet several times over. We do

not need troops on foreign soil if we do not intend to

meddle in their affairs. That solves the military deployment

problem. With regard to economic investment by the

United States Government, we bring our equipment,

supplies and people back home to provide goods and

services within our own borders. Let the foreign host have

the land and facilities. Concerning foreign investments by

American capitalists, they must decide where they wish to

live. If they want to stay with their foreign investments,

they should be free to do so. If they want to live in the

United States they can liquidate their investments and

come home. They could also leave their investments in

place and let local people manage them as long as they

understand that the US military is not going to protect

investments on foreign soil. It should be extremely difficult

to enter the United States and very easy to get out. Suppose

there existed only one nation and one government on

Planet Earth and the United States was that nation and that

government. That would be the utopian society everyone

dreams about including the radical liberals. In such a world

where only the United States exists, why would we need or

be concerned with other nations? If other nations want to war upon each other either economically or militarily let them do so. However, if you want to attack the United States, be prepared to meet your God."

Bill could not refute the general's cold logic. "Well stated, General. We have to pause for a short break and then hear from our other guests."

Following the commercials, Bill turned to Colin Coldfish. "Colin, as White House Chief of Staff, can you explain to me Osama's political strategy in surrounding himself with confessed socialists, vocal communists, ex-convicts, tax cheats, and black militants?"

Colin was taken back by the direct and unambiguous accusation from Bill. "I think you may be overstating a couple of instances of bad judgment that are being corrected. The president is dedicated to delivering on his campaign promises and to selecting the motivated individuals to support his efforts. The president has been

unfairly attacked by right wing extremists who will sink to

any level to discredit his monumental achievements."

Bill exerted great effort to remain civil. "What Osama

has done screams so loud at me I cannot hear any thing he

reads from his teleprompter. It is true he has a great gift. He

can read another person's words in a persuasive way which

sounds so good that you don't initially realize he is directly

attacking the fundamental concepts upon which this

democratic republic was founded and prospers. You speak

of his monumental achievements. I do not know of any

monumental achievement on his part other than getting

himself elected president in spite of being foreign born,

having forged official documents, associated with hard

core communists, publicly stated his allegiance to Muslims

rather than Americans, lied about his campaign financing,

and supported flagrant voter fraud on the part of Forenborn. As a matter of fact, he taught Forenborn recruits how

to perpetrate voter fraud."

In spite of his cool demeanor, Colin's cheeks turned a

little pink. "Those are all unfounded and malicious charges

with no foundation in law or fact."

Bill smiled with delight. "Well, Colin, lets review some

recent revelations:

"Osama's paternal grandmother says he was born in

Kenya. A Honolulu newspaper reported on January 8, 2006

that he was born outside the United States. In an October

2004 political debate Osama admitted he was foreign born.

A Harvard classmate testified that Osama told him he was

born in Kenya. The Kenyan Ambassador to the United

States stated that Osama was born in Kenya. Hospital

officials in Mombosa Kenya say Osama was born in their

hospital. Two local Christian ministers signed affidavits

that Osama was born in Mombosa, Kenya. He has spent a

cool million dollars or more on legal fess and expenses to

keep from producing an official birth certificate. In his own

writings he admitted to being mentored by a communist

and acknowledged that his father was a communist. He

also personally admitted to seeking out Marxist professors

and friends while attending college. He sought endorse-

ment by hard core socialists, domestic terrorists and black

militants. He has personally admitted these associations

and chose a domestic terrorist to ghost write one of his

books. He applied as a foreign student for financial aid at

Occidental College in California. He flew to Pakistan on a

foreign passport when it was illegal for Americans to travel

to Pakistan. He appointed to cabinet posts four confessed

tax cheaters. He appointed to positions as Czars a dozen

individuals known to be either socialist or communist and

very much anti-free market and anti-capitalism. He was

personal friends with slumlords and con artists --- all of

whose backgrounds were investigated, verified and

broadcast by Glen Ripuone on Telitright News. Each of

these alleged statements and events has been carefully

investigated and documented by Telitright News. You will

have to do more, Colin, than resort to name calling and

Saul Alinsky type ridicule to convince our viewers that

these accusations are unfounded."

Bill was finished listening to Colin's attempts to

whitewash Osama. He turned his attention to Timmy

Notax.

"Timmy, have you gotten around to paying your tax

bill? Now that you are Secretary of the United States

Treasury, will you get the other Osama appointees who

cheated on their taxes to pay up?"

Timmy swallowed hard to keep from choking on his

tongue. "Actually, Bill, I truly believed I had filed my

return correctly. I used Turbo Tax computer software and

had my accountant check the numbers before I filed the

return. It was an unintentional error. As for anyone else

who filed an incorrect return, they will indeed pay any

taxes owed to the IRS."

"It appears that you guys who are being investigated all

used the same accountant. Or, perhaps you loaned out your

Turbo Tax software. In any event, I find it hard to swallow

that someone who cannot figure out his own tax liability is

now in charge of the IRS." Bill smiled with open

contempt. "Is the Osama administration about finished

picking the taxpayers' pockets to bail out UAW and the

morons managing the U.S. auto industry? Who's next? The

ultra liberal newspapers?"

Timmy knew he was playing with fire. He dared not

antagonize Bill Smiley. "The taxpayers will be repaid with

interest. Until such time that the loans are repaid with

interest, the taxpayers will own stock in each debtor to

secure the loans. Our primary objective was to save jobs

and help turn the economy around."

"What if the debtors blow the money and turn belly up?

I don't recall the taxpayers being consulted about taking

such astronomical risks."

Bill got the cue that his time would expire in thirty

seconds. "Thank you, Gentlemen, for a very interesting

show. If you are inclined to come back, we will talk more

about what Osama and his liberal Congress are trying to

accomplish."

The President of Russia Ivan Putinmeon and his Prime

Minister Vladamir Stalinsky were hosting Venezuela

Dictator Hugo Makuslav in the Kremlin diplomatic hall. .

Ivan studied Hugo over the rim of his glass of vodka. The

big bellied, pancake faced, yellow skinned Venezuelan

Indian was personally repulsive to Ivan. However, Hugo

had hammered the Venezuelan people into submission and

had earned some menial measure of respect.

He wanted more Russian military hardware and was

therefore willing to cooperate with Russia on diplomatic

issues and stonewalling the United States in South

America. Ivan was short, swarthy and well proportioned

with mousey features, short brown hair and piercing dark

eyes. Vladamir, on the other hand was short, slender, and

looked like a male fashion model with hand tailored black

suit, gleaming white shirt, blue tie and expensive black

leather shoes. He gave the impression of a smooth Russian

statesman.

Ivan drank the bottom of his glass and set it noiselessly

in front of him while looking directly into Hugo's black

eyes. "What can you pay for, Mr. President?"

Hugo locked his hands over his doughy stomach. "300

short range missiles, 50 MIG fighters, 500 armored

vehicles and 50 tons of assorted munitions." Vladamir

smiled wryly. "According to the last G20 conference, that

would stretch your national treasury somewhat."

"Perhaps we can soften the price a bit," Ivan suggested.

"Your personal power of persuasion in forming a coalition

among your neighbors to vote with us at the UN could

lower your weapons cost to accommodate your budgetary

limits."

Hugo's eyes sparkled. "I am now working out that

strategy."

Vladamir picked up his pen and began taking notes. He

looked up at Hugo with obvious mirth. "You may want to

convert your dollars to rubles. The United States is devalu-

ing the dollar with irresponsible and unprecedented

spending to force a socialist takeover in America. I would

gamble on U.S. bankruptcy before the end of Osama's

term. The eagle is fast becoming a sparrow."

Ivan refilled their glasses while gazing sideways at Hugo. "When your term is up, go to America and run for the White House. By then the socialists will be looking for a new face. You certainly don't have to worry about being foreign born."

Senators Barney Smirk, Joe Flipover, Harry Heapiton, Maggie Getsome, Charles Rakitin and Chris Gimmie conferenced with Speaker of the House Nancy Tearieye behind closed doors. Nancy was flustered.

"We're still three votes short in the House on Healthcare and we're behind schedule. It's time for some serious arm twisting. Let's hear it from Louisiana."

Maggie Getsome, Senator from Louisiana was a political whore, opportunist and greedy pig. She saw a chance to sell out the American people for a granddaddy back room deal for her state. Bringing home the government freebies would keep her seat warm.

"Madam Speaker, I don't feel that this bill is going to benefit the people of Louisiana to the point that I can support it. However, I am willing to discuss my concerns with you in private."

Chris Gimme raised his snout from the public trough and studied Nancy. He knew exactly where she was headed and he wanted a piece of the bribe pie. The two-faced dingbat had her political career riding on the healthcare bonanza for her supporters who generally paid no income tax and were parasites on American society. Nancy had become accustomed to robbing the taxpayers to further her political ambitions. She certainly did not want to sit home in the Napa Valley and watch illegal aliens pick her grapes. Another trillion or two added to the national debt didn't seem to concern President Osama or Timmy Notax. Why not grab a hundred million or so while the Speaker was in the bribing mindset?

"Madam Speaker, I also have a couple of questions I need answered before I cast my vote.."

"Certainly," Nancy responded. "I'll make time to see each of you after lunch today." Nancy began to relax a little. She knew what the price would be for each vote and Osama would not stand in her way. Maggie would get on board for funding of her three hundred million pet project in Louisiana and Chris could be bought for a hundred million as long as his vote was fully committed before Maggie got diarrhea of the mouth.

Osama's motorcade sped along the streets of downtown Boston. The black Muslim knight from Mombosa was fuming. What was going on with his fickle supporters? Didn't they understand he was their true Messiah? He would rule them with benevolence and Islamic wisdom inherited from his father. The fat cat bankers and wall street tycoons would be forced to ante up to support his socialist agenda. Couldn't even the simple minded in Massachusetts get it? Didn't they understand he was going to take from the rich and give to the poor? He definitely had more pressing business than holding Lillie Legal's hand. Serving as Attorney General for Massachusetts, she should have captured Killer Cain's senate seat by a landslide. Now, he would have to wow the most faithful liberal Democrats in America with his brilliance and humor to atone for her ineptness. She was down in the polls running against an unknown Republican. He would blow the guy away with sarcasm, ridicule and a timely touch of humor. The Great One would not be denied the senate seat in Massachusetts. Even a distinguished liberal senator suggested the Democrats in Massachusetts should vote ten times.

Osama exited his limo and strode like a Muslim cleric to the rally platform amid a scattering of cheers from blind followers. His heart fluttered as he noticed the sparse crowd. Where was the party machine? There had better be a lot of dead people voting if the Democrats expected to overcome a seven point lead by the Republican challenger.

He smiled and waved through his introduction with the arrogance of an Arab sheik throwing gold coins to mindless rabble.

His pitch for Lillie followed the same finger pointing oratory that he had repeated so many times that he didn't have to read from his teleprompter. The Republicans were getting in his way while he swept up after former President Hush. His healthcare plan would be passed into law. He was going to create or save ten million jobs. His green energy projects were going to turn the economy around just as soon as he finished cleaning up behind the Republicans.

His confidence wavered when hecklers shouted him down for a full three minutes. He joked about the heckling and continued explaining the mind boggling mess he had inherited. But, things were coming along. Monumental improvements were just around the corner. He needed a loyal supporter to fill Killer Cain's seat. The people of Massachusetts should unite and never allow such a revered senate seat to be filled by an obstructionist Republican. He resorted to some more ridicule and mocking of the Republican candidate and then hurried on his way to very pressing presidential business.

The liberal news media praised Osama's stump speech like words of wisdom spoken by Lincoln, Jack Kennedy and Martin Luther King all rolled into one by the most intelligent and gifted orator of the ages. What a fabulous president he had become being so dedicated to lifting up the poor and oppressed. There would be ladders of opportunity for them to climb out of poverty. He gave them so many thrills up their legs just by his majestic presence.

The dollar kept falling in the currency market and the stock market followed suit. Osama's threat to levy a special penalty tax against the banks created more market uncertainty. What would this foreign born Muslim demagogue dream up next. Perhaps a tax on swimming pools and hot tubs?

China and Japan began planning mass conversion of dollars into Euros. Senior citizens on fixed incomes lost another ten percent of their purchasing power and began converting their retirement savings into gold and other precious metals. World stock markets became shaky. Recent small gains in the market vanished.

CHAPTER EIGHT

Osama's political adviser David Yurnany and Federal Reserve Chairman Maury Printsome were welcomed by Willie Watchem and nervously sat down for an anticipated pummeling.   David and Maury had been pressured by Osama to accept Watchem's invitation to appear on his show and promote the White House and Congressional agendas. Telitright News enjoyed skyrocketing ratings and Osama felt that the mushrooming millions watching Telitright needed to hear the truth for a change.

Willie directed the first question to Maury: "Mr. Federal Reserve Chairman, what is different today within the den of thieves controlling the Federal Reserve Banks?"

Maury's jaw quivered with uncertainty. The history of

the Federal Reserve System had been hidden from the

American Public for more than seventy years. How much

did Willie Watchem know?

"I'm not sure what you are referring to. Are you

suggesting our Federal Reserve System does not serve the

best interest of the American People?"

Willie looked holes in Maury's forehead. "That is

precisely what I am saying. Let's take a few minutes and

educate our viewers on the history of the Federal Reserve

Banks and one of the most slimy and dishonest presidents

America has endured other than Barry Osama. I am

speaking specifically of Franklin Delano Roosevelt and his

fellow criminals and con artists. So, again I ask, Mr.

Chairman of our Federal Reserve System, what has

changed among the den of thieves? Aren't the same

families the owners of the New York Federal Reserve Bank

as well as the other Federal Reserve depositories? Doesn't

private ownership of the Federal Reserve banks demon-

strate how easily greedy politicians and the American

president can pilfer the taxpayers' money. Moreover, those

individuals who own the Federal Reserve Banks can get

even more filthy rich by inside information on the Fed's

interest rate for investment banks. Then, there is the ugly

history connected with the Rothchilds, the Rockefellers,

and other opportunists who own the Federal Reserve

financing Fascist, Nazi, socialist and communist dictators

in order to raid the assets of foreign governments. Ameri-

can taxpayers should be nauseated by the American

corporations profiting from both sides of several wars by

funding our enemies and selling the materials and

technology to kill our troops. Osama, the liar, forger and

thief plus the radically liberal Democrats have absolute

control our trillions of taxpayers' dollars. What, Mr.

Chairman, is going to stop Osama and his fellow thieves

from stealing us blind?" Maury Printsome dared not say he

would protect the taxpayers' money because Willie would

then ask how he would go about stopping such mass

thievery. "American citizens must rely upon the integrity

of the system with its built in checks and balances." Willie

chuckled. "When you have the entire government including

all appointees controlled by liars, forgers, tax cheats,

domestic terrorists, and demagogues, there are no checks

and balances. The fox is now guarding the hen house,

Maury. Our Chief Law Enforcement officer is a mental

case who pardons terrorists and provides citizenship rights

and paid lawyers for terrorists caught trying to bomb

jetliners and public places filled with civilians. He also

sends them to civilian courts where bleeding heart liberal

judges can turn them loose on some minor technicality.

Our intelligence agencies have to read them their rights and

furnish them with lawyers prior to questioning. Our Congress is filled with abortionists, evolutionists, thieves, and

homosexuals. Our president is a natural born African

Muslim with ideology. So, who is going to keep this

Osama from pilfering the public treasury?" Maury knew

Willie was right about the absence of morality within the

Osama administration. They were radical socialists without

a trace of any conscience whatsoever. Osama taught Saul

Alinsky Rules for Radicals which disavows any sense of

morality. Yes, indeed. The public treasury was in great and

imminent danger.

"I think this concern needs to be addressed by the

United States Treasury Secretary, Timmy Notax."

Willie snorted. "I'm sure that tax cheat will do his fair

share of pilfering. Tell us, Maury, is the United States

bankrupt?" Maury tried to dodge the question. "We have

amassed a huge debt fighting two wars and bailing out the

banks and auto makers. Such massive debt will have to be

spread out over a couple of generations, but it will be

repaid."

Willlie did not back off. "How, Maury? There is not

enough money on planet Earth to pay our current national

debt plus our unfunded entitlement programs. After taking

on the commitment to shoulder the non-collateralized

derivatives dumped on the American taxpayers, the United

States is insolvent. We owe more than we can pay. In

economics 101, Maury, that is called bankruptcy. A bank-

rupt nation is not a favored candidate for receiving loans

from other nations. That means, Maury, that the dollar is

going to become worthless in the foreseeable future. That

is also known as the Cloward-Piven strategy for destroying

capitalism and collapsing our economy thereby forcing in

anarchy and pushing the American population into a

socialistic global government. That strategy, Maury, is

precisely what Osama taught the recruits at Forenborn.

That is what Osama and Georgie Sorrow are conspiring to bring about during Osama's communistic and dictatorial administration. Osama and Georgie are being assisted in the destroy America campaign by greedy pigs in Washington and intellectually handicapped Hollywood personalities who live out pretend lives."

Maury had no comeback and Willie pressed him. "The soon to be majority of voters in America do not have sufficient education to realize they are trading their freedom for communistic slavery. They are going to become very hungry, Maury. After the capitalists flee the United States, there will be no one left to pay taxes to feed them while they sodomize each other, smoke dope, demonstrate against our constitutional freedoms, conceive and murder babies. The one positive aspect of the fall of America is that our thrill up their legs, radically liberal and socialistic media, our slimy Congress, our judicial imbeciles and the man from Mombosa may well face a

bloodthirsty and starving mob that will tear them apart like

plucking a chicken for the frying pan. Personally, Maury, I

hope that hungry mob becomes cannibalistic and eats their

sorry carcases."

Willie turned his attention to Osama's personal consult-

ant, David Yurnany. "Tell me, David, isn't it a fact that

Barry Osama taught Alinsky's Rules For Radicals to

Forenborn recruits including the Cloward-Piven Strategy?

And, David, isn't it also a fact that the former Cloward-

Piven gangs of thugs and racist agitators founded the

Forenborn community organizer concept to threaten, bully,

and coerce officials into socialistic agendas?"

Yurnany shuddered inwardly, not from these two

questions but from what he knew was to follow. "President

Osama has dedicated his life to lifting up the oppressed and

underprivileged. After graduating from Harvard, he did

teach Forenborn recruits for awhile. However, he matured

into a position in the Illinois Senate where he could better

champion the cause of the working class. Now, as

President he is empowered to transform this nation into a

society where all citizens have an equal chance to become

financially successful and provide a decent standard of

living for their families."

Willie had to breath deeply to keep from throwing up.

"That is pure unadulterated propaganda conceived for the

specific purpose of deceiving the citizens living on

taxpayer funded welfare into believing that they can

continue living off another person's sweat and individual

incentive while enjoying the good life evolved from

monkeys."

Willie looked into the cameras and frowned. "Thank

you gentlemen for coming and thank you faithful viewers

for watching. I have some personal thoughts to share with

you after a commercial break."

Willie reappeared after the commercial break and smiled into the cameras. He was seated at his conference table with his hands folded in front of him. "I want to summarize for our viewers what we have covered during the past several shows. We have challenged the hypocrisy of the sitting Congress and the communistic agenda of President Barry Osama. Our primary concern is the bankrupting of America and the conspiracy to propel this nation into a global government by destroying our economy."

Willie voice reflected his patriotic pride. "Because Americans are kindhearted, generous and peace loving; black demagogues, racial agitators, socialists, communists, and the Barry Osamas among us are crying for redistribution of wealth, the end of capitalism and the free market in favor of a one world government where social parasites can suck the blood from those providing the necessities of life on Planet Earth. Well, this wondrous utopia of redistribution of wealth has been tried before and every time the result was disastrous. During the first century A.D. the early Christian church experimented with communism and found that even among devout followers of Jesus Christ it doesn't produce harmony for those who work to feed those who don't such that the Apostle Paul finally proclaimed that those who do not work shall not eat. The Pilgrims who landed at Plymouth Rock tried redistribution of wealth by having all things in common and nearly exterminated themselves. Only when each Pilgrim enjoyed the fruits of his/her own labor did the colony become self-sufficient and manage to survive the second winter."

Willie paused, sipped some water and continued. "And, of course even those who were never taught actual

American history instead of homosexuality and evolution will remember the famous Russian effort to make communism work which brought about the dissolution of the Soviet Union. While Barry Osama was smoking dope and swearing to be a foreign student from Kenya and Nancy Tearieye was learning how to exploit illegal aliens, they managed to miss out on our American history and constitutional safeguards. They want to live like Arab sheiks while the laboring taxpayers share their income with the lazy, the shiftless, the welfare sponges, and the domestic terrorists among us. Barry Osama's allegiance is to the Muslim jihad and his terrorist brothers. Nancy uses illegal aliens to work her vineyards and rips off the taxpayers for a private plane to jet around the country spreading communist ideology. Barry Osama's military genius is displayed by foot dragging on troop deployments while his terrorist brethren regroup and rearm themselves.

Such has been his total contribution as our military Commander-in-Chief."

Willie next summarized some historical facts. "Okay, for the historically illiterate and the willingly ignorant, here is a five minute lesson in American history that traces the rise and fall of America:

"Our forefathers founded this nation upon Christian principles and values. At the time of the signing of the Declaration of Independence approximately 98% of the American population were professing Christians as opposed to around 76% today and the Holy Bible was used as a text book in our public schools. Because we honored God and the teachings of Jesus Christ, our ragtag thirteen colonies with an inept military, limited arms and resources, and plagued with British Loyalists throughout the colonies, defeated the greatest military power in the world in 1776 to establish an independent and free republic supported by capitalism, the free market system, and personal freedom to succeed or fail financially in proportion to individual effort and ingenuity with God and Jesus Christ as our guiding light."

Willie was not bashful concerning his moral perspective. "Thus by 1960, a brief 184 years, we rose from obscurity to the greatest economic and military power that has ever existed. The only possible explanation for this meteoric rise to world dominance is our Christian founding and reverence we gave to God and our burning desire to spread the Gospel of Jesus Christ. Now, I ask the intellectual evolutionists, sodomites, tax cheats, and abortionists among us: What is your alternate explanation? Did we sodomize and murder our children to become a great nation? Perhaps we enjoy such prominence by trying to feed and care for those among us who are able to work but won't? Or maybe we just succeeded beyond the wildest imagination of oppressive dictators because we like baseball and apple pie."

Willie now expressed the obvious. "I submit that the left wing radicals who are tearing down our nation through legalizing abortion, sodomy, child infanticide, homosexual seduction in our public schools, and a one world communistic dictatorship cannot explain the phenomenal rise of the United States to world dominance within three lifetimes other than by the divine providence our forefathers relied upon. America survived the insane economic policies of Woodrow Wilson and Franklin D. Roosevelt, two definite socialists, by being thrust into two world wars which taxed America's industrial might. When JFK was assassinated, we inherited Lyndon B. Johnson's 'great society' wherein we became hippies, indulged in unbridled illicit sex, began murdering our children in the womb, opened the closet for homosexuals and child molesters, decided that God is an intrusion upon our free choice, and decided it is more prudent to spend more on welfare sponges and less on maintaining our military. We forgot, in less than one generation who we are, our Christian heritage, our self-reliance, our morals and family values, and decided that we are more enlightened than God and therefore He can take a hike." The main camera switched to a facial close-up of Willie as he ended his monologue. "In exchange for barring God from our public life and continuously blaspheming Jesus Christ and his teachings, we got Barry Osama, Nancy Tearieye, Harry Heapiton, Barney Smirk, and a communistic White House administration determined to convert the United States into a beggar nation. We now owe, including our unfunded welfare entitlement programs, 117 trillion dollars. That, folks, in case you struggle with math, is one and a half times the combined gross national product of every nation on Earth. We are in a suicidal economic free fall which will end in national bankruptcy, the abandonment of our military for lack of funding, and massive devaluation of our currency. That, my friends is the rise and fall of America.